Winner's Circle Crosswords

Tyler Hinman

To Perrin Tingley, David Christie, my family, and all the other adults who helped foster a kid's unusual hobby.

An Imprint of Sterling Publishing
387 Park Avenue South
New York, NY 10016

PUZZLEWRIGHT PRESS and the distinctive Puzzlewright Press logo are registered trademarks of Sterling Publishing Co., Inc.

The puzzles in this book originally appeared in the TASIS Echo (at TASIS England American School) and Statler & Waldorf (at Rensselaer Polytechnic Institute) from 1999 to 2006.

ISBN 978-1-4027-8820-8

Distributed in Canada by Sterling Publishing
c/o Canadian Manda Group, 165 Dufferin Street
Toronto, Ontario, Canada M6K 3H6
Distributed in the United Kingdom by GMC Distribution Services
Castle Place, 166 High Street, Lewes, East Sussex, England BN7 1XU
Distributed in Australia by Capricorn Link (Australia) Pty. Ltd.
P.O. Box 704, Windsor, NSW 2756, Australia

For information about custom editions, special sales, and premium and corporate purchases, please contact Sterling Special Sales at 800-805-5489 or specialsales@sterlingpublishing.com.

Printed in China

2 4 6 8 10 9 7 5 3 1

www.puzzlewright.com

CONTENTS

INTRODUCTION

Welcome to "Winner's Circle Crosswords"! The 82 puzzles in this volume are 13 squares wide and 13 squares tall (except for the unusual one on page 74), which is slightly smaller than the traditional 15×15 grids you might be accustomed to seeing in your weekday newspaper. I hope you'll find them every bit as entertaining!

This book holds a great deal of nostalgia for me. Aside from some polishing here and there, I constructed these puzzles during my high school and college years. I was in ninth grade when my history teacher introduced me to the New York Times crossword during study hall, which ignited a long series of events that has changed my life far more than I could have imagined. Over the several years following that fateful afternoon in late 1998, I became a full-blown puzzle addict. On a whim, I started making my own crosswords, and strove to hone my skills as both a solver and a constructor.

My efforts in puzzlemaking paid off on July 4, 2000, when my first New York Times crossword debuted. I was 15 years old. It was a tremendous thrill, which spurred me not only to try to sell more puzzles but also to continue showing off my work to my peers. Part of me felt at home in a 13×13 grid, and creating puzzles remained a part of my routine throughout high school and my entire college career. I'm very happy to bring these creations to a wider audience.

If you flip through the book, you'll see some additional text next to the grids, and that's where the solving half of my crossword life comes in. As my construction skills were getting better, so were my solving abilities. A month after I started doing the Times crossword every day, the Tuesday edition (the second-easiest puzzle of the week) was still giving me fits. But I didn't give up, and after a year of practice, I was able to solve thorny Friday puzzles. I wanted more of that gratifying sense of improvement, so I began to solve more puzzles (and to time myself on the easier ones). I started attending the American Crossword Puzzle Tournament, and I jumped from 101st place in 2001 to 19th place in 2003, winning a B Division title; that's when I knew that taking first place and becoming the youngest-ever champion had to become my goal. With heaps of training and a healthy dollop of luck, I captured the trophy in 2005 at the age of 20. It was the culmination of an immensely satisfying journey, and alongside the puzzles in this book, I share the knowledge I picked up along the way. I hope they will boost your accuracy, your speed, and your enjoyment of crosswords.

Happy solving!

—Tyler Hinman
www.tylerhinman.com

HARD AT WORK

ACROSS

1 Relaxed sounds
4 Foot part
8 They're thrown
12 Those with Y chromosomes
13 ___ Straits
14 It's clicked
15 Like some screams
18 Former unit of money in Florence
19 ___ layer
20 Bonus
22 Plenty
26 Guns, as the engine
30 Tame
31 Engage in an extremely strenuous workout, say
36 Exclamation before "Who goes there?"
37 Den
38 Banishment
40 Indian king
45 Texan stronghold
49 Binary star in Lyra
50 '80s British music group
54 Put away, as a suit
55 Bring to the ground
56 Fault line?
57 One of the Great Lakes
58 "Then again ..." on the web
59 Match (a bet)

DOWN

1 Walk leisurely
2 Double ___ (17-Down's shape)
3 Indication of contempt
4 Throw in
5 Puerto ___
6 Santa ___, California
7 Kind of sandwich
8 Quandary
9 Here, to Pierre
10 Disadvantage
11 Language in this puzzle: Abbr.
16 Canoe item
17 See 2-Down
21 Creative works
23 ___ rally
24 Hawaiian memento
25 Heart test: Abbr.
27 90° bend
28 By way of
29 Tackle the slopes
31 Female pronoun
32 Opposite of wane
33 New Haven collegian
34 On the lam
35 Make a mistake
39 Ernie of golf
41 Blvd. kin
42 Blue ___
43 Concur
44 It makes waste
46 Style that's far from close-cut
47 Castle protector
48 Pasta whose name means "barley"
50 Henry VIII's middle name?
51 It has a canal
52 "The Phantom Menace" boy, for short
53 Disdainful expression

Don't get locked into

an incorrect answer.

ANSWER, PAGE 90

TAKE A BOW

ACROSS
1 Dog sound
4 A gardener might pull one
8 Dundee dances
12 It's three, four, or five, usually
13 Fabled race loser
14 Surname of a baseball dynasty
15 First half of a punny quip
18 Fifth noble gas
19 What kids on vacation have?
20 Places with many cages
22 Green Day song on "Dookie"
23 One piece of a colored candy
26 Word before stop or grinder
30 Writer from Baltimore
31 Sweet potato
33 Southern school, or the name of its mascot
34 Gave a boost
37 Crossword clues, sometimes
40 Internet string
42 Film holder
43 Take back
47 Fat flier
50 Second half of the quip
52 Rum drink
53 It has prongs
54 Self-esteem
55 Get a glimpse of
56 Goes downhill, say
57 ___ sheet

DOWN
1 Top
2 Wild party
3 Wild
4 "What the heck!"
5 Dine
6 Dundee's home
7 Free versions of computer games
8 One who throws people in the slammer
9 "Casablanca" character
10 Says, in teen slang
11 Tries to get money from, in a way
16 Cheer (for)
17 Second
21 Clever
23 Place to relax
24 Fish in a pond
25 Corny item?
27 He had lots of travels
28 Period of history
29 Rapper who's the son of a jazz musician
32 Russian space station
35 Funeral speech
36 Add to a hand
38 Fixes, as a computer program
39 Sandwich place
41 Speaking problems
43 Road ___
44 Screws up
45 ___ circle
46 2008 Penn portrayal
48 Prefix with byte
49 Stage item
51 ___ vive

If you have one answer

sitting in a corner,

ANSWER, PAGE 90

KEEPING TRACK

ACROSS

1 Biblical twin
5 Prefix with system
8 Questions
12 ___ liquor
13 Damage
14 It may be guilty
15 First half of a humorous quip
18 Start up again, as a business
19 Emulate a fish
20 Levin or Gershwin
21 Dog on "Frasier"
24 Lost city
29 Noted work?
30 Ghost's cry
31 Factions
33 Cure for baldness?
34 Coffee pots
36 Large reptiles
38 ___ end (gridiron position)
40 Long time
41 Matches, in poker
43 Heart parts
47 Second half of the quip
50 It can't move diagonally
51 Original sinner
52 Refer to
53 Match components
54 Join
55 Prop for an animal stunt

DOWN

1 Mideast bigwig
2 "Ditto"
3 To boot
4 More work?
5 Gives out
6 Four-wheeler
7 Spheres
8 Pests on 16-Down
9 Lose weight
10 He's a doll
11 Melancholy
16 Flowerless plants
17 Meadow mother
22 "What's ___ for me?"
23 They may be eaten raw
24 Border on
25 Amos or Spelling
26 It just might pay off big
27 It's crushed or cubed
28 Watched without downloading, as a video
32 "Spy Hard," for one
35 Arab chiefs
37 Supplement
39 X
42 Like lines that are neither parallel nor intersecting
44 Threesome
45 About
46 Put one's foot down?
47 Org. with an April deadline
48 Water tester
49 "___ done it!"

and you can't get anything else to work with it,

revisit that answer.

ANSWER, PAGE 90

AS EASY AS ...

ACROSS

1 ___ Lanka
4 Apollo org.
8 Faucets
12 It sometimes precedes a groan
13 Cartman's first name, on "South Park"
14 Where 47-Across is
15 Half of a sequence
18 Where to throw a ball around
19 New: Prefix
20 Payment
21 Count's end?
23 ET's craft
25 Untruths
28 Bleeped, say
33 Elevator innovator
34 Eggs
35 Latvia's capital
36 One advancing rapidly
38 English school
39 Summer drink ending
40 Station that shows Bronx Bombers games
42 One on the diamond
44 Had a bite
47 Thailand's neighbor
50 Other half of the sequence
54 Not active
55 Teen's bane
56 67.5° direction
57 Got ready to drive, with "up"
58 Greek letters
59 Actor Beatty

DOWN

1 Health place
2 Red gem
3 Ancient Peruvian
4 Has to have
5 Pound sound
6 Portent
7 Result of a strenuous workout
8 ___ Mahal
9 Tread on thin ice
10 Heap
11 "___ here"
16 Clad
17 Debt acknowledgements
22 Aberdeen resident
24 Anticipated
25 Haze
26 Simpson trial judge
27 New York, with "the"
29 Rapper who had a UPN sitcom
30 Not (a one)
31 Trip taker?
32 Quarterback Marino
37 Eye drop?
41 Workshop workers
42 Part of a course
43 À la ___
45 Pre-1917 ruler
46 Use acid, maybe
48 Buffoons
49 Part of a New Year's song title
51 Mathematician's abbr.
52 Colorful card game
53 "Men in Black" boss

Pen vs. pencil is overrated.

1	2	3	■	4	5	6	7	■	8	9	10	11
12			■	13				■	14			
15			16					17				
■	18				■	19			■	20		
■	■	■	21		22	■	■	23	24		■	■
25	26	27		■	28	29	30				31	32
33				■	34			■	35			
36				37				■	38			
■	■	39			■	■	40	41		■	■	■
42	43		■	44	45	46	■	47		48	49	■
50			51				52					53
54				■	55				■	56		
57				■	58				■	59		

I usually go with pen in the news-paper, just because it's smoother,

ANSWER, PAGE 90

GOING DOWNHILL

ACROSS

1 Windows relative
4 Rip off
7 Word with syrup or leaf
12 "Shoo!"
13 Investment plan: Abbr.
14 Extraterrestrial
15 Sign of bad weather
17 Was violent
18 Most crowded
20 Loses traction
21 Throw randomly
23 Manners
25 Debt write-up
26 French river
28 Grimm character
34 Responded to the alarm
35 14-Across's craft
36 Make a pit stop
38 Feudal system land divisions
40 Woman's wear
41 Eyes
44 Earn
46 Good at
49 "Common Sense" pamphleteer Thomas
50 Low noise?
51 Part of a royal flush
52 Lose one's lap?
53 Have
54 Coniferous tree

DOWN

1 Frisbee catcher
2 "___ Mutual Friend" (Dickens novel)
3 Bowl
4 Putting in peril
5 Mine finds
6 First, second, or third
7 Drink with an olive
8 In the style of
9 Football
10 West Yorkshire city
11 Football positions
16 100 sen
19 Inflict a heavy blow, biblically
21 Douglas, for example
22 Baseball great Gehrig
24 Electric swimmer
26 Word that can follow the key word in this puzzle
27 Tee preceder
29 Faux ___
30 Suddenly spewed
31 Fat ___
32 Small boat
33 Figures: Abbr.
36 "Superb!"
37 Ventricles' neighbors
38 Con
39 Fury
40 Spends little (on)
42 One to rub noses with
43 Deal with snow
45 Hotel
47 Hockey player's milieu
48 Word in advertisements

but I use a pencil when

I'm solving puzzle books like this one.

ANSWER, PAGE 90

KUDOS

ACROSS
1 They have nuclei
6 Massage locale
9 Small green vegetable
12 Fortune teller's deck
13 Krueger's street
14 Fink
15 Newspaper supplement
16 "Great!"
18 Amusing act
20 Sign in a store window during the day
21 "Great!"
24 Ripped
25 In the past
26 Toy with a wrinkled face
27 Possesses
28 "Why do I care?"
30 End neighbor
33 Cooking vessel
34 ___ good deed
35 Chess great Mikhail
36 One of Henry VIII's wives
38 "Great!"
40 Colored part of the eye
41 Ballroom dance
42 "Great!"
44 Nimble
48 Ball holder
49 Woodsy ___
50 At no time
51 Fool
52 Language suffix
53 Washer's partner

DOWN
1 Cleaned one's plate
2 Charge
3 Morsel
4 Ethical
5 Refuse to abandon one's beliefs
6 Doing needlework
7 It's behind win and ahead of show
8 Novelist Tan
9 Ask for one's hand in marriage
10 Zealous
11 Make up (for)
17 Add
19 Show off
21 Existed
22 Self
23 Supermarket's claim
27 It might be worn during a workout
29 Gymnastics apparatus
30 Unpleasant destiny
31 Black stuff
32 Large deer
34 What takes you halfway home?
36 One of a trio of ships
37 The ram
38 Blossoms
39 Gamble
43 Baseball great DiMaggio
45 ___ League
46 Confederate general
47 Misjudge something

Make sure the answer's part of speech matches the clue.

If the clue is [Flavorful]

ANSWER, PAGE 90

OFFBEAT

ACROSS
1 Pronoun for a ship
4 Experiment rooms
8 Be humorous
12 Hang back
13 A Baldwin brother
14 Where products are on display
15 Whatever
16 Radius's neighbor
17 Erupt
18 First half of a George Carlin quip
21 Tiny meower
22 Hawks
24 Emanations from a bakery
27 Prepare, as a dinner table
28 Agile for one's age
31 Take home
32 Word sung twice after "Que"
33 "You ___ here"
34 Jackson hit
36 Squander
38 Outfits
42 Second half of the quip
45 Giver's word
46 Sea movement
47 19th Greek letter
48 Land of the green
49 Nights before
50 With
51 Last letters
52 Track competition
53 ___ sauce

DOWN
1 Not taut
2 Vietnam's capital
3 Suez Canal country
4 One who praises
5 Like some tool kits
6 Curve
7 Quickly read
8 Outlaw James
9 Profit diminisher
10 Traffic cop's quarry
11 Haul (away)
19 Command to a dog
20 "Idiot boxes": Abbr.
23 Train stop: Abbr.
25 "Give ___ break!"
26 Present one
28 It has teeth
29 Grassland
30 Bring back
32 ___ poker
34 Sleeping place
35 It measures the ability to learn
37 Multiplied by
39 Smidgens
40 It may be grand
41 Hit the books
43 List part
44 Plunge
45 Tasseled hat

the answer will be another adjective like TASTY,

not merely a related word such as STEAK.

ANSWER, PAGE 90

IN THE MONEY

ACROSS

1 Flow's partner
4 Important tests: Abbr.
8 Roman emperor
12 Chum
13 Grow weary
14 Using speech
15 Winter driving hazard
16 Got off
17 Wallace of "60 Minutes"
18 Quick money back?
21 Upset, with "off"
22 Do away with, with "of"
23 Hum
25 It's in the doghouse
26 Waxed winter item
29 Like someone who loves money?
33 Pt. of 23-Down
34 Seven, to 8-Across
35 Shakespearean betrayer
36 Gradually drink
37 Pay (up)
39 Deserved money?
44 Green gem
45 ___ table
46 Important time
47 Therapeutic plant
48 White-tailed bird
49 Did a sprint
50 Sharp cry
51 Require
52 It has a pupil, but is not a teacher

DOWN

1 Long poem
2 German composer
3 Emulating a goat
4 Actor's milieu
5 Was sick
6 The Musketeers, for example
7 Liberate
8 Wandering one
9 Idle of Monty Python
10 Leaf mover
11 Spanish cry
19 Unpopular one
20 Pocket bread
23 International gp. headquartered in Geneva
24 "And I Love ___" (Beatles song)
25 21st Greek letter
26 "Don't move!"
27 Fraternity party fixture
28 Statement of commitment
30 Not good
31 Eagerly deal with a present
32 Middle neighbor
36 Important thing to get
37 Having a tendency (to)
38 Fixed, as gears
39 Bundle
40 Worshiped thing
41 Golfer's warning cry
42 It's carried in the lunch room
43 Having all one's marbles
44 Blue ___

If you're stuck, take a break.

It's amazing how the mind continues to

ANSWER, PAGE 90

APT ANAGRAM 1

ACROSS

1 Spots on TV
4 Troubles
8 Cape Canaveral org.
12 "Just kidding!"
13 ___ mater
14 Skunk's weapon
15 Apt anagram of 45-Across
18 Diplomatic representative
19 Friendless one
20 Salon selections
21 Long times
22 Web
25 Arousing
27 Flip
29 Not there
32 Eats away at
33 A little wet
34 Big drink holder
35 Cooking instrument
36 Small land
38 Las Vegas numbers
42 Hot chocolate
44 Powerful chess piece
45 Apt anagram of 15-Across
48 Lieberman was his running mate
49 Largest continent
50 Always, in verse
51 Wagon pullers
52 It's put into a mouthpiece
53 Deli choice

DOWN

1 Fed the kitty
2 Brand of fabric softener
3 Martin of "The Man With Two Brains"
4 Like some hair
5 Bullring cry
6 Use
7 Hair ___
8 Facial feature
9 Made beautiful
10 Mama's boy
11 "You ___ here" (words on a map)
16 Gambling damages
17 Needing to use a lifeline on "Who Wants to Be a Millionaire," say
21 Add-on to a telephone number: Abbr.
23 L.A.-to-N.Y. dir.
24 Football scores: Abbr.
26 Tempt
28 Holey
29 Current unit
30 Fluffy scarf
31 True
32 Farm female
34 Go by
37 Detection instrument
39 Dissuade
40 ___ Decimal System
41 Annoying night noise
43 Kitchen appliance
44 Thigh muscle
45 Personality part
46 Salmon
47 "That's a ___!" (accusatory phrase)

attack the problem even when you're

not looking at it or consciously thinking about it.

ANSWER, PAGE 90

WE'VE GOT IT ALL

ACROSS

1 What an air ball misses
4 Storage unit
8 Opera singer Gluck
12 Keats creation
13 It starts in the corner
14 ___ duct
15 Like many children
18 Not quite snow
19 Italian for "two"
20 Nub
23 Blush-inducing
27 Was hospitable toward, say
30 ___-Ball
32 "Get out!"
33 Object of ridicule
36 Annoying spots
37 Prefix with 4-Across
38 Plane heading: Abbr.
39 Angle symbol, often
41 Mood indicator
43 ___-mo
45 Ones with 36-Across, much of the time
49 Easy things to shoot
54 Crossworder's favorite cookie?
55 Staff start
56 Chopper
57 Covenant
58 Foil alternative
59 Norm: Abbr.

DOWN

1 Knocks over
2 "American ___"
3 Nothing more than
4 Americans' allies
5 Hither's partner
6 Auto club service
7 ___ out a living (scraped by)
8 Minimally
9 MGM's logo
10 It doesn't do Windows
11 Ancient refuge
16 Subzero: Abbr.
17 Knight
21 Like some milk
22 Belief system, either way you read it
24 "___ on first?"
25 MDs
26 Link together
27 Not natural, maybe
28 A pop
29 Sand ___
31 Waffle brand
34 Goes on a winning streak
35 Southwestern capital
40 Boxing family name
42 Poetic contraction
44 Not never
46 History book chapters, say
47 Waiting room call
48 It races down and is dragged back up
49 Dandy
50 Nest egg: Abbr.
51 "Hang on a ___!"
52 Mont Blanc, for one
53 Spelling or quilting event

A puzzle's clues are taken in through the eyes, not the ears.

Puzzle makers will sometimes exploit this and try to fool you.

ANSWER, PAGE 90

WHERE IT'S AT

ACROSS

1 Prepares for battle
5 "Where ___?" (disoriented person's question)
8 ___-worth
12 Froth
13 Silent assent
14 Pay for
15 Racing sled
16 Menu style
18 Famed barbarian
20 It may get stubbed
21 Small task
25 Question
28 Actress Long
30 Prod
31 Get sick, in a way
35 Fall (over)
36 Religion that worships the Three Pure Ones
37 Eminem's music
38 Gets angry
41 Former fast flyer: Abbr.
43 In any situation
48 So to speak
51 Type of exam
52 CI × VI
53 Register, as grievances
54 Unseen "Cheers" character
55 Takes out
56 Vied (for)
57 A loop doesn't have any

DOWN

1 G sharp equivalent
2 17–0 score in baseball, say
3 Wise ones
4 Extract metals from
5 Californian city
6 Burrowing creature
7 Gem State
8 Draw no cards
9 Muff one
10 Tennis do-over
11 Destiny
17 Chewable stuff
19 Make amends (for)
22 Du ___
23 Stew ingredient
24 Tone
25 Boats like Noah's
26 Edible fat
27 It has a cap
29 In the proper place
32 Lost island
33 Not of the Americas
34 Thorned thing
39 Tend to the grass
40 Smudge
42 Treasure ___
44 Heart chambers
45 Small bird
46 Tough to crack
47 Reference book
48 Throw in
49 Form of jazz
50 "___ Got a Secret"

1	2	3	4	■	5	6	7	■	8	9	10	11
12				■	13			■	14			
15				■	16			17				
18				19						■	■	■
■	■	■	20			■	21			22	23	24
25	26	27	■	28		29	■	■	30			
31			32				33	34				
35				■	■	36			■	37		
38				39	40	■	41		42	■	■	■
■	■	■	43			44				45	46	47
48	49	50						■	51			
52				■	53			■	54			
55				■	56			■	57			

If a clue won't break, **perhaps you're mentally pronouncing a word the wrong way.**

ANSWER, PAGE 90

APT ANAGRAM 2

ACROSS

1 Foggy
5 Sharp punch
8 Electric current units
12 Not toward the wind, at sea
13 Individual
14 Team ___ (San Jose Sharks fans)
15 Christmastime
16 Shaky
18 Apt anagram of 41-Across
20 Sea eagle
21 Gain, as weight
24 One of four areas
29 Motion of the ocean
30 Start to cycle?
31 Says indistinctly
33 Tex-___
34 Humble response to praise
36 Most serpentine
38 N'awlins sandwich
40 Tumult
41 Apt anagram of 18-Across
47 Places to tread
49 Ancient Peruvian
50 Painter of a melting clock
51 Hexa- half
52 Continue
53 Freelancer's encl.
54 Game bird
55 Possesses

DOWN

1 Group of cards, and what you use to hold it
2 Soothing succulent
3 Final letters
4 Barked
5 Diaries
6 "___ and the King"
7 #1
8 Went to a restaurant
9 Part of GMT
10 Where to take notes
11 Crafty
17 Reward for waiting
19 Makes a mistake
22 Poetic exultations
23 Adjacent (to)
24 Bon mot
25 "Render ___ Caesar ..."
26 Hoopsters' embarrassments
27 Religious woman
28 Swaps for an upgraded model
32 Peel
35 Certain terrier
37 Rainbow color
39 "That's gotta hurt"
42 Place to tread
43 She describes herself as "poor, obscure, plain, and little"
44 Falling flakes
45 Computer image
46 Gets some sun
47 Pt. of WPM
48 Towers?: Abbr.

Watch your letter patterns.

If you have a bunch of consonants strung together in an unlikely pattern, check your crossings.

ANSWER, PAGE 90

ON THE EDGE

ACROSS

9 River that's 4,187 miles long
10 Supergroup with albums called "Aqua," "Aria," and "Aura"
11 Golfer Greg
13 Of the skin
15 "Now ___ seen everything!"
16 Direct
18 It's made from taro root
19 Place for eggs
21 Anger color
22 Mercedes-___
23 In court
25 Blender setting
26 WWW address
27 For every
28 Ease up
31 In an impressive manner
34 Apiece
35 ___ Lanka
36 Group of three
37 Baseball stat
38 One of the Great Lakes
40 Flightless bird
41 Atone for something, with "oneself"
43 One with a book
45 "___ Rock"
46 Small branch

DOWN

1 Agitation
2 That guy
3 "Woe is me!"
4 Of the belly side
5 Fatigued
6 Exploiter
7 Respectful address
8 Mess (with)
12 Kitchen fixture
14 Of the highest quality
17 It may be electric
20 Fact
22 Charred
24 Strong anger
25 It's in a pod
27 Before
29 Talking pig in the movies
30 Like a substance with a low pH
31 Dog's warning
32 Uncover, with "up"
33 Green fruit
35 Poison ___
38 Prefix with sphere
39 Current info
42 Hammer's location
44 Broadcast

However, constructors sometimes try to include

longer entries with uncommon letter sequences, so beware.

ANSWER, PAGE 91

APT ANAGRAM 3

ACROSS

1 Wander
5 Country singer McEntire
9 Lie
12 πr^2, for a circle
13 Chunks of history
14 Single
15 One of Henry VIII's wives
16 Shopping ___
17 Dusting item
18 Apt anagram of 41-Across
21 Curse
22 Takes it easy
24 Sign of winter
29 Blue hue
30 Baseball score
31 "Come in"
33 Seventh Greek letter
34 Prefix with graph
36 Become irked
38 Noise of contempt
40 Simile words
41 Apt anagram of 18-Across
47 High degree
48 Baseball legend Berra
49 Wild party
50 "I didn't know that!"
51 Fungus
52 Nights before
53 Use +
54 Fencing sword
55 TV rooms

DOWN

1 Emulates Eminem
2 Kind of exam
3 Dynamic opening?
4 Mrs. Washington
5 Taking it easy
6 Guitarist Clapton
7 Gala
8 Up and about
9 Envisions
10 Confused
11 Implore
19 Simple
20 Sandra Bullock film, with "The"
23 Wooden strip
24 Liberal ___
25 Satisfied, as thirst
26 Dropped off
27 Shoshonean Indian
28 Reserve
32 Ferrous oxide
35 Hospital rooms: Abbr.
37 Put two together
39 Herb used as incense in ancient Greece
42 Roller coaster feature
43 Leer at
44 Church area
45 Tied
46 Jam
47 Golfing org.

If one section of a puzzle is eluding you, but you have

one or two tentative answers in your head, write them in.

ANSWER, PAGE 91

THE SOUND'S THE SAME

ACROSS

1 Beat in chess
6 Black sticky stuff
9 Down time
12 Strong adhesive
13 North or South follower
15 Y
17 Betelgeuse and Rigel's location
18 First or second
19 Catherine of British history
22 Former Mauritius natives
24 Leave
25 In ___ (actually)
26 Electrician's unit
29 With 31-Across, Wye
31 See 29-Across
33 NNW opposite
34 Goes out
38 It's forbidden
39 Win all the games
40 Cozy
41 Assistant
44 Battle
46 "Why?"
51 "Cool!"
52 It's red, yellow, or green
53 Inedible, maybe
54 Join, in a way
55 Actors' aspirations

DOWN

1 Brooks or Gibson
2 Primate
3 Tater ___
4 Gets wrongly, in a way
5 One changing hair color
6 They're forbidden
7 Sets right
8 Striped one
9 Piece of old Italian bread?
10 They may have hearts
11 Stare
14 Holds up
16 Fairground attraction
19 Church benches
20 They're used to 30-Down
21 Irritate
23 Opposite of 'neath
26 Cosmetics company
27 Restaurant list
28 ___ rock (music genre)
30 Cut down
32 Fit
35 Turned into
36 Sang loudly
37 Fight a little
39 Stitches
41 Not closely
42 Hawkeye's home
43 Got ready to fire
45 Playful creature
47 Question word
48 Spot for a facial
49 Obsolete
50 Classic video game system: Abbr.

If any letter is right, seeing it in place could make another answer jump out at you.

1	2	3	4	5	■	6	7	8	■	9	10	11
12					■	13			14			
15					16							
■	■	■	17					■	18			
19	20	21		■	22			23		■	■	■
24				■	25				■	26	27	28
29				30	■	■	■	31	32			
33			■	34	35	36	37	■	38			
■	■	■	39					■	40			
41	42	43		■	44			45		■	■	■
46				47						48	49	50
51							■	52				
53			■	54			■	55				

ANSWER, PAGE 91

LOOK THE OTHER WAY

ACROSS
1 Bowling bane
6 Beer holder
9 Shock physically
12 "Me, Myself & ___"
13 Prefix with skeleton
14 ___ trip
15 Nary a soul
16 Take a load off
17 Rouen refresher
18 Alternate title for this puzzle
21 Works in English class
23 Look of derision
24 Gym unit
25 Jumped
28 What this puzzle salutes
34 Gin's partner
35 It's rolled
36 Wall painting
39 Tranquilize
42 Alternate title for this puzzle
45 Family
46 Large tub
47 Very large
50 Yale collegian
51 War winner, most of the time
52 Young horses
53 Comfy room
54 Took the front
55 Destinies

DOWN
1 Ball stand
2 Lodge
3 Dancer's garment
4 College teachers, familiarly
5 Trig ratios
6 Attend
7 Lighted sign
8 Small falcon
9 Vanity item
10 Once more
11 Laughs at
19 Divulge
20 Prefix with copter
21 Sneaky one
22 Affirmative
26 Nanki-___ (character in "The Mikado")
27 Caption in a weight loss commercial
29 Lowest of the low
30 Restricted
31 Rare food
32 It may be cherry or apple
33 Promos
36 Ulyanov of politics
37 Spry
38 Did an autumn job
40 Hair twist
41 One of many in a supermarket
43 Go for the gold
44 Flattened circle
48 Feather scarf
49 Switch position

Tougher puzzles will

exploit words with two or more meanings.

ANSWER, PAGE 91

READ ALL ABOUT IT

ACROSS

1 Decorate glass
5 Vexes
9 James Bond, e.g.: Abbr.
12 Sailor's greeting
13 Profound
14 Mongrel
15 Protect oneself
17 George Gershwin's partner
18 Italian city that lends its name to a color
19 Accelerate
21 Noah's boat
23 It has teeth
24 Golf goal
27 First name in "The Godfather"
29 Bashes into
32 Spooky
35 Regarding
36 Gambling game
37 "Just kidding!"
38 Pelts
40 Chap
42 Schulz's comic
45 One of Bart and Lisa's aunts
49 Everyone
50 Canadian emblem
52 Under the weather
53 Soft cheese
54 Idle
55 Middle word in an Elvis title
56 ___ cost (free)
57 Like some lines

DOWN

1 Has a meal
2 Asian cuisine
3 Pepsi rival
4 It might be laughing
5 Wedding words
6 Guns, as the engine
7 "Don't stop now!"
8 Fling
9 Ecological problem
10 Wise guy
11 Golf hazard
16 Prepare, as a turkey
20 Viscount's superior
22 Get going, as an old motorcycle
24 It had eleven states: Abbr.
25 Good things
26 Concealed holes
28 Common article
30 6 letters
31 Army rank: Abbr.
33 Example, for example
34 Parasite
39 Cuban dance
41 Gets someone's attention, say
42 Beach toy
43 Fitzgerald of jazz
44 "Wheel of Fortune" option
46 Give out, as confidential information
47 Labyrinth
48 Some
51 The lion

Take time to consider all the angles

on a clue that's baffling you.

ANSWER, PAGE 91

REREAD ALL ABOUT IT

ACROSS
1 Indian king
5 Jeff MacNelly comic
9 View
12 Got off
13 Wildcat
14 It has four wheels outside and one inside
15 Bit of creativity
17 In the past
18 Revolutionary Guevara
19 Poem whose title might start with "To"
20 Tempted
22 Attacks
24 Clothes
25 Advance in baseball, possibly
28 Rummy goal
29 Floor above the ground
32 Give (in)
33 Opportunities, figuratively
34 Makes better
36 He had the world on his shoulders
40 Three-card ___
41 ___-Air
43 Six-foot runner
44 First lady
45 Make sleeping arrangements
48 Homework helpers, often: Abbr.
49 "You got that right"
50 Part of A.D.
51 Table scrap
52 Tennis divisions
53 Cribbage pieces

DOWN
1 ___ dressing
2 Hilo hi
3 Does a certain dance
4 Enjoyed food
5 Lost traction
6 Jekyll's alter ego
7 I
8 Glorify
9 More creepy
10 With gusto
11 Wore away at
16 Numbers game
21 Maximum
23 Mountaineer's progress
24 Too
26 Goals
27 Stir
29 Urn
30 Most balanced
31 Singsong syllables
32 Awoke
35 Liabilities
37 Sierra ___
38 With
39 "Super Duper ___" (animated series)
41 Fight
42 ___ out a living (scrapes by)
46 Mine find
47 Blame

Most crosswords have a healthy dose

of trivia amidst pure word knowledge.

ANSWER, PAGE 91

THAT SPECIAL SUM THING

ACROSS
1 Metrical unit
5 Puncher
8 Recipe direction
12 Cuisine with pad see ew noodles
13 Big ___
14 Drive-___
15 Aimed at
17 20 quires
18 Dr. ___
19 Make happy
21 Genie's master
23 Shocking swimmer
24 Worn away at the edge
25 ___ On-Line (King's Quest game company)
29 Morning moisture
30 Many, many years
31 Haphazard
35 Ideally
38 Flock female
39 Silly talk
40 What may exert peer pressure?
42 Black gunk
43 Stead
44 Sort of
49 Guinness who played Obi-Wan Kenobi
50 Cycle beginning?
51 First murder victim
52 Fringe benefit
53 ___ Antonio
54 Skirt variety

DOWN
1 Addams family cousin
2 "Got it!"
3 Feb. follower
4 Adam Sandler movie
5 Go to
6 Suffering
7 Shelves
8 Have between one's legs
9 You, once
10 Persia, after 1935
11 It's distilled from fermented molasses
16 Canal or lake
20 Hawaiian gift
21 Field
22 It surrounds a house
24 New Deal pres.
26 Film holder
27 Got up
28 It's red or black
32 Doomed one
33 Be in debt
34 Deserves
35 Reach
36 Start of a Christmas rhyme
37 Nightmare
40 Digestive fluid
41 Look (at) suggestively
43 Once around
45 Gun gp.
46 Bulls' org.
47 Form datum
48 Manning of football

Since trivia clues tend to have a you-know-it-or-you-don't nature,

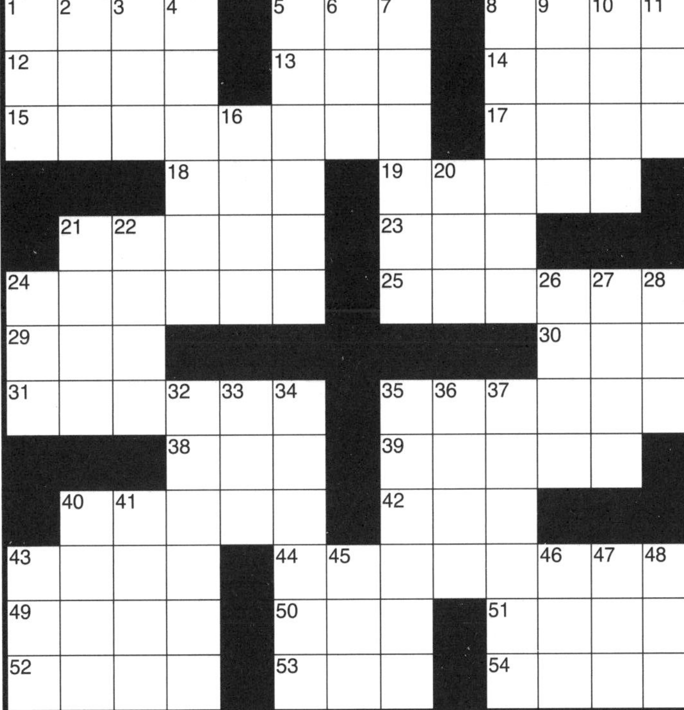

focus on vocabulary-based clues when trying to break into a difficult area.

ANSWER, PAGE 91

2-H CLUB

ACROSS
1 Light brown
5 Night sky sight
9 Fast food 21-Across
12 Whirled
13 Bard's tributes
14 Morpheus's ally
15 Lip
16 Keep
18 Surround
20 Shaft
21 See 9-Across
22 Pres. who served for the most terms
24 Funny people
25 Challenged to a duel
29 Evian, for one
30 "Gotcha"
32 Great anger
33 Anticipate
35 Bolshevik leader
37 V + V
38 Respond to pain
39 Guinness or Baldwin
42 Pest related to the lobster
43 Tacklebox item
46 "Excuse me!"
49 Band aid?
50 Roof overhang
51 Place
52 Straight line from a point
53 Small bird
54 And others: Abbr.

DOWN
1 Curvy letter
2 Tax expert: Abbr.
3 Tucker/Chan comedy
4 Displace
5 Bad kind of situation to be in
6 Norse deity
7 Dog doctor
8 Fire leftovers
9 Fort of gold
10 Chop down
11 Cryptogram, say
17 Dwell (on)
19 Utilize improperly
21 "See ya!"
22 Winter illness
23 Central American flower
24 One wearing stripes
25 Female pronoun
26 Appear later in the game, maybe
27 Creepy-sounding lake
28 Hideout
31 Layer?
34 Do some engraving
36 Put in a container
38 No longer asleep
39 From a distance
40 Peruvian capital
41 Athlete's award
42 Wander
44 Chop down
45 Rowing necessity
47 7th of 24
48 Gibson or Brooks

If you try only the occasional crossword when you happen to see one in the paper, consider what day it is.

ANSWER, PAGE 91

Many sources ramp up the difficulty as the week progresses;

CASE STUDY

ACROSS

1 Advice for tackling this puzzle?
4 &
7 Ask for money, say
10 Light beam splitter
12 Buck's mate
13 Hawaiian souvenir
14 Italian seaport
15 Wren building, familiarly
17 Most adorable
18 X
21 What a pizza might be split into
23 Meet by chance
25 Rube
28 Enthusiasm
29 Role on "The Drew Carey Show" and in "La Bohème"
30 Power units
32 Looks up to
34 Revisit, as an idea
36 37-Down victim
37 Actress Stone
39 Imply
41 One form of water
45 Start of a sequence
46 Big hole
47 Site of a 1945 conference
48 Bartender who serves Homer and Barney
49 Large expanse

DOWN

1 Computer picture ext.
2 Suffix with press
3 Bad thing
4 Annoyances that pop up on the Internet
5 Nick
6 Sheriff's ally
7 Sign of a nice day
8 They have no ventral fins
9 Essence
11 Whiz
16 In
18 ___ cut
19 Hip-moving dance
20 Spellbound
22 He's done for
24 Young worker, possibly
26 Austen heroine
27 Thpeak like thith
31 Ice cream units
33 ___-turvy
35 Start to remove, as shoes
37 Something fraudulent
38 Bum
40 Pilot's announcement: Abbr.
42 Inventor Whitney
43 Cash dispenser
44 Actress West

Monday is gentle while Saturday is a real brute.

Sunday tends to be somewhere in the middle of that range, but it's bigger.

ANSWER, PAGE 91

CHRISTMAS EVE SCHEDULE

ACROSS

1 Information
5 Spun trap
8 Really impresses
12 Harvest
13 ___ standstill
14 Alaskan town
15 Initials on a pre-1991 map
16 Started, as a conversation
18 6 P.M.
20 Get rid of money
21 Hardly stringent
25 8 P.M.
29 "I've got it!"
32 Sound heard during fireworks
33 Sock ___ (dance)
34 10 P.M.
39 Stealing
40 Buenos ___
44 Sometime after 10 P.M. (if at all)
48 Item in a police file
51 Croft of Tomb Raider
52 Balm ingredient
53 Previously
54 Get to work on Time?
55 Company Steve Jobs started after leaving Apple
56 Dandy
57 They color

DOWN

1 They may be over-the-counter
2 Moral man
3 Sample
4 Cooks' garments
5 Get clean
6 Words from Caesar to Brutus
7 Roseanne's last name
8 Heavy thing on a ship
9 Chinese cooking vessel
10 Australian bird
11 It may be represented by 9: Abbr.
17 West Coast campus
19 401, to Flavius
22 Sound heard during fireworks
23 ___-mo replay
24 Psychic power
26 Oriole's local rival, for short
27 Group of whales
28 X, on a fraternity house
29 Appropriate
30 "Come again?"
31 Enjoyed a meal
35 Compensate for
36 Mormons settled it
37 Spanish article
38 Was very successful, as a comedian
41 Prepared
42 Creepy
43 Petty quarrels
45 Thumb (through)
46 Building block
47 At the summit of
48 Tried to steal a base
49 Warm-fermented stuff
50 Old curse

The first word of a clue is capitalized as a style convention.

1	2	3	4	■	5	6	7	■	8	9	10	11
12				■	13			■	14			
15				■	16			17				
18				19						■	■	■
20					■	■	■	21		22	23	24
■	■	■	25		26	27	28					
29	30	31	■	■	32			■	■	33		
34			35	36				37	38	■	■	■
39					■	■	■	40		41	42	43
■	■	■	44		45	46	47					
48	49	50						■	51			
52				■	53			■	54			
55				■	56			■	57			

Constructors write tricky clues that exploit this.

ANSWER, PAGE 91

REARRANGEMENTS

ACROSS

1 Cenozoic, Paleozoic, etc.
5 %: Abbr.
8 "What ___ is new?"
12 Miniscule
13 Boat tool
14 Repast
15 New Testament book
16 It will get a pitcher ejected
18 STOP
20 Before, to a bard
21 Slippery one
22 SPOT
26 POST
30 Not the morn
31 Puts in the overhead compartment, say
34 Friend in the 'hood
35 TOPS
37 OPTS
39 U.S. Navy rank
42 Mont Blanc, for one
43 POTS
49 Did better than
50 Get exactly right
52 Double reed
53 Hor. opposite
54 Itch
55 Lines of fashion?
56 Road curve
57 Hang in the balance

DOWN

1 Greek vowel
2 Loaded
3 Start to freeze?
4 Method
5 Most swanky
6 Cod, for one
7 Group of natives
8 Preserve, in a way
9 Disclose, as confidential information
10 Store event
11 Building wings
17 Italian crowd?
19 Baseball Hall of Famer Speaker
22 Acoustic unit named for Alexander Graham
23 Hawaiian neckwear
24 The last word?
25 Ad ___ committee
27 Focus of some workouts
28 Rage
29 ___ Angeles
32 Hockey team that became the Hurricanes
33 Convinced
36 There are five (but some claim to have six)
38 "Unlock this door!"
40 Large degree
41 Push
43 Hundred Acre Wood denizen
44 Service a car, in a way
45 It's very 12-Across
46 Some bills
47 Not often seen
48 Yield, for one
51 Took the front

A common example is [West of Hollywood] for MAE,

referring to Mae West and not a direction.

ANSWER, PAGE 91

PIECEWORK

ACROSS
1 Mister, in Munich
5 Cleopatra's undoing
8 Swear
12 Light bulb, figuratively
13 Word after spelling or quilting
14 Prom transport
15 Bite (on)
16 Laughs
17 Onion relative
18 Tough chess piece?
21 Where the smallest bone is
22 Mess (with)
23 C-sharp equivalent
26 Strong tree
27 College extension
30 Captured chess piece?
33 Sucker
34 Choose
35 Use an épée
36 Praising work
37 ___ 41 (punk band)
38 Passive chess piece?
44 Sticky situation
45 "Yes, Captain!"
46 Noted ark-itect?
47 ___ again
48 Wrath
49 Stupor
50 Erode
51 Poppycock
52 Originate (from)

DOWN
1 Up there
2 ___ St. Vincent Millay
3 Bum
4 Definitely not a bargain
5 Loathe
6 Scorch
7 Old Spanish capital
8 Get rid of, as fears
9 Look at
10 Black cat, possibly
11 Chinese fryer
19 ___ ray
20 Laugh (at)
23 Music players
24 Org. concerned with planes
25 Sass
26 Not safe
27 Almost forever
28 "What's up, ___?"
29 Hawaiian instrument
31 Alfresco
32 Nudges
36 Wiser, they say
37 ___ shooting
38 Cosecant's reciprocal
39 Cuzco valley dweller
40 Novice
41 Capricorn
42 Torture, as a pledge
43 Our enemies
44 Acknowledge applause

Take heed of question-marked clues; wordplay is afoot!

For these, don't waste time thinking about what the phrase conventionally means.

ANSWER, PAGE 91

SHIFT HAPPENS

ACROSS

1 Where the answer to this clue is located ... or is it?
4 Policeman's alert
7 Chunk of gum
12 Plant pest
13 Frequent joke setting
14 Conceit
15 Hanging sight
17 Left over
18 Word before shift
19 Word before shift
21 It will make you cry
23 Astronomy pioneer
27 Fall, in a way
29 Caller?
30 Makes a sum
31 It comes in and goes out
33 What 4 may signify
34 Jesters
35 Appear
38 Man, for one
39 Understand
40 Small noise
42 It smells
44 Good thing
47 Word before shift
50 Word before shift
52 Adjusted (to)
53 West Indies republic
54 Chaotic place
55 Univ. reward
56 Take up space
57 Sixth sense

DOWN

1 Opp. of WSW
2 "Snug as ___ ..."
3 It's usually rectangular
4 Escape
5 Drenched
6 Ancient
7 Put on
8 Word in dates
9 Indicate
10 Selfish one
11 Suffix meaning "sort of"
16 The Red Wings, on scoreboards
20 Take up space
22 Tax org.
24 Friend
25 North American river
26 Not working
27 Annoying one
28 Speak gratingly
32 Foil's relative
33 Affects
35 Not many
36 Conditionals
37 Tastelessness
41 Numbers games
43 Ostrich's kin
45 "Saturday Night Live" specialty
46 Eager
47 Barely beat
48 Ship's pronoun
49 Be difficult
51 Jr.'s son

Try to figure out other ways the words could be read

1	2	3	■	4	5	6	■	7	8	9	10	11
12			■	13			■	14				
15			16				■	17				
18				■	19		20			■	■	■
■	■	21		22				■	23	24	25	26
27	28		■	29				■	30			
31			32		■	■	■	33				
34				■	35	36	37		■	38		
39				■	40				41		■	■
■	■	■	42	43				■	44		45	46
47	48	49			■	50		51				
52					■	53			■	54		
55					■	56			■	57		

and what those new interpretations might imply.

ANSWER, PAGE 92

OH, C, CAN YOU SAY?

ACROSS
1 ___ chop
5 Seemingly limitless
9 Media monitor: Abbr.
12 It's tied
13 Montreal baseballer, formerly
14 Baseball legend Gehrig
15 SEA
18 Dogs, cats, birds, etc.
19 Mover's load
20 It may be flexible
23 Dickens's alias
24 SEE
30 Fleming who created James Bond
31 It's all around you
32 Plague
33 CEE
38 Rower's tool
39 Hank who hit 755 home runs
40 Tax cheat's nightmare
43 Young horse
45 SÍ
50 Tater ___
51 Nifty
52 Two-toned treat
53 Start of a googol
54 Has the rights to
55 Int'l. org.

DOWN
1 Penultimate Greek letter
2 Resistance unit
3 CD-___
4 Pursue relentlessly
5 It has no sleeves
6 Fires
7 Therapeutic place
8 She doesn't play with dolls
9 Rate of flow
10 Dessert holder
11 Coaches make them
16 Salamander
17 Seep thickly
20 Do laps
21 Bangkok tongue
22 Author Ayn
23 Titanic sinker, for short
25 Balding loss
26 German article
27 Practice in the ring
28 Extinct bird
29 Wagon pullers
34 Slay
35 Hispanic-American
36 Guys' partners
37 Betrays, say
40 Regarding
41 Abreast of
42 Dinner, say
43 Jackie who does his own stunts
44 Cereal ingredient, often
46 Make clothes, in a way
47 Time to remember
48 Ball stopper, sometimes
49 As well

If the question-marked clue is for one of the longest entries in the puzzle, it's probably a theme answer and you'll need

1	2	3	4	■	5	6	7	8	■	9	10	11
12				■	13				■	14		
15				16					17			
■	■	■	18				■	19				
20	21	22			■	■	23			■	■	■
24					25	26				27	28	29
30			■	■	31			■	■	32		
33			34	35				36	37			
■	■	■	38			■	■	39				
40	41	42			■	43	44			■	■	■
45					46					47	48	49
50			■	51				■	52			
53			■	54				■	55			

ANSWER, PAGE 92

FIT TO BE TIED

ACROSS

1 Busy person in Apr.
4 Blue ___
8 Cleans, in a way
12 Give a hand to
13 Base truant
14 Opera showstopper
15 Sashaying and such
18 Farming pioneer
19 Super ___ Osborne
20 Cost
21 Take effect
23 Fagin's gang
25 Person in an old yearbook
29 Highlander or Lowlander
30 Place for a quick note
34 Iona College athlete
35 5-Down sounds
36 Communion and confirmation, for two
38 Theme of this puzzle
43 Doesn't use moderation
44 Hautboy
48 Translucent stone
49 English landmark
52 Nose wrinkler
53 Arthur, Herbert, Julius, or Leonard
54 "I like ___"
55 Something to hit in Guitar Hero
56 Not elated
57 Winter hours in Chicago: Abbr.

DOWN

1 Flings
2 Outburst
3 Scolder, most often
4 Shock
5 Shocked
6 Frank Oz character
7 Croat or Serb
8 Big ___
9 Hole of a sort
10 Want desperately
11 Best, as advice
16 Smith role
17 Inexperienced
22 Refresh oneself, say
24 Shakespearean killer
26 Ringo's john
27 Thing shrouded in mystery
28 Dash datum: Abbr.
30 Got hitched
31 "I'd prefer we do something else"
32 Bit of land in France
33 "Don't ___"
34 Become more appealing to
37 Bad sea signal
39 A 1-Across deals with many: Abbr.
40 ___ nerve
41 Springs a leak?
42 Not quite snow
45 Shocking, unexpected news
46 Not written
47 Light color
50 "Forgot About ___" (Eminem song)
51 Chopper

a few crossing answers to figure out what's happening.

Don't spend too much time on one of these if it's blank.

ANSWER, PAGE 92

THAT'S THE SPIRIT!

ACROSS

1 Head hillbilly of classic TV
4 Don't make use of
9 Restaurant seating option
12 Chopping tool
13 More under the weather
14 Korean car
15 Confusing
17 Lay of Enron
18 Urban problem
19 Flight datum: Abbr.
20 Bonus, at work
21 Singer Janis
23 Not often
25 Put down in writing
28 Having difficulty
31 Unit in history class
32 Entity making mischief five times in this puzzle
34 Bush, in college
35 Dramatic scene
37 "Green ___"
39 It's spun
40 Menu words
41 Big lug
43 Brilliant performance
45 Panda's food
49 Einstein's birthplace
50 Follow-up injection
52 Adversary
53 Like a nose, sometimes
54 Roman greeting
55 Stole
56 David of "Just Shoot Me"
57 Tough spot to leave, often

DOWN

1 Some punches
2 Final, for one
3 Downloadable version, usually
4 Ace
5 "The Curse of the Jade Scorpion" star
6 Skirt feature
7 Bodily connectors
8 One dyne per centimeter
9 One crunching numbers
10 Rank
11 Home run champ Aaron
16 Get down
20 They have Windows
22 Rags-to-riches writer
24 Of birth
25 It hits the net
26 George's collaborator
27 One in a big generation
28 Promise to pay
29 Cheer in Spain
30 Poetic contraction
33 Ends a conversation, in a way
36 Technological layout
38 Alternatives to buses
40 Make better
41 Aficionado
42 Moises or Felipe of baseball
44 Europe's highest volcano
46 One-legged character
47 "Don't just sit there!"
48 Ejected
50 Obnoxious folks
51 Deli supply

1	2	3	■	4	5	6	7	8	■	9	10	11
12			■	13					■	14		
15			16						■	17		
18				■	19			■	20			
■	■	■	21	22		■	23	24			■	■
25	26	27			■	28					29	30
31			■	32	33				■	34		
35			36				■	37	38			
■	■	39				■	40			■	■	■
41	42			■	43	44		■	45	46	47	48
49			■	50				51				
52			■	53					■	54		
55			■	56					■	57		

After you solve enough puzzles,

Just practice!

ANSWER, PAGE 92

ON THE UP AND UP

ACROSS

1 Dash (down)
4 Bobby on the Food Network
8 Gift tag word
12 Time
13 Be imminent
14 Major marriage place
15 Price to pay
16 Ox attachment
17 Over
18 Agitate
20 One of a 15th–century threesome
22 "H-e-double-toothpicks!"
23 Skin condition
26 Times
28 0
30 Airport abbr.
31 Lummox
32 Plan that may be rolled over: Abbr.
33 One of Pooh's hundred
34 "Blah, blah, blah": Abbr.
35 Cinch
36 Chickened out, in a way
37 Item in an English book
39 ___ avis
41 Sacrifice, maybe
42 Out there
45 Aloe ___
47 Fill to excess
49 Neither's partner
50 "Sounds fine to me"
51 Biblical victim
52 H
53 What Spider-Man shoots
54 Clotheshorses
55 Waterway construction

DOWN

1 Goldblum of "Independence Day"
2 Treat that turned 100 in 2012
3 Beef up?
4 Lara ___ Boyle
5 Screw up?
6 Good to go
7 Hook up?
8 "NYPD Blue" actor
9 Brush up?
10 More than 28-Across, barely
11 Cut down, in a way
19 Bridge position
21 Diamonds, informally
24 Female horse
25 Let go
26 He played Obi-Wan
27 Roman Empire invader
29 "... man ___ mouse?"
33 Disco Stu's style
35 Enjoy the beach, say
38 Wharves
40 Lutzes' kin
43 Bit
44 Prepare desperately (for)
45 Altar words
46 Barely get, with "out"
48 Blood classification system

you'll start to get a feel for how constructors and editors think,

1	2	3	■	4	5	6	7	■	8	9	10	11
12			■	13				■	14			
15			■	16				■	17			
18			19			■	20	21			■	■
■	■	22				■	23				24	25
26	27			■	28	29			■	30		
31				■	32			■	33			
34			■	35				■	36			
37			38			■	39	40			■	■
■	■	41				■	42				43	44
45	46			■	47	48			■	49		
50				■	51				■	52		
53				■	54				■	55		

as well as for the vocabulary that comes up in puzzles most often.

ANSWER, PAGE 92

THEMELESS CHALLENGE 1

ACROSS

1 Hack
4 Screw up
8 Wile E. Coyote's brand of choice
12 Bud's comic partner
13 Ice cream holder, maybe
14 Show one's teeth
15 Cruising
18 Board
19 The ram
20 Big key
22 Settles
25 Poi source
27 English logician with a diagram
29 Female of the flock
30 Ideally, it's never used
33 Signal of approval
34 Is, in Spain
35 They'll move you
36 Tennessee player
38 Wives' quarters
40 Reserved
42 Roddick who founded the Body Shop
45 "Oh, big shocker"
48 Sprayer
49 Formations in the sky
50 Drum's place
51 Goes (for)
52 Place to get stranded
53 Unexciting

DOWN

1 Dancing shoe
2 Top quality
3 Breakfast fare
4 Bloodhound's clue
5 Londoner's stop
6 Like an aside
7 One who may exert pressure
8 Be harmonious
9 Grilled, maybe
10 Actress Farrow
11 Word after tight or loose
16 ___ roll
17 Fool
21 December 24 and 31
23 One may be fraternal
24 Match components
25 It's pitched
26 Mine, in France
28 Final Four org.
31 What rubbing may yield
32 Makes flush
37 Chips in
39 Employee's request
41 $IV^{IV} - C$
43 Rend
44 Haywire
45 "Horton Hears a ___"
46 Quick trip
47 Shocker underwater

"Cross-wordese" is the term for answers that appear all-too-often in puzzles

1	2	3	■	4	5	6	7	■	8	9	10	11
12			■	13				■	14			
15			16					17				
18					■	19					■	■
■	■	20			21		■	22			23	24
25	26			■	27		28		■	29		
30				31					32			
33			■	34				■	35			
36			37		■	38		39			■	■
■	■	40			41		■	42			43	44
45	46						47					
48				■	49				■	50		
51				■	52				■	53		

but very rarely in anything else.

ANSWER, PAGE 92

DON'T COUNT ON IT

ACROSS

1 St. Louis hrs.
4 Captain's ___
7 Word said twice in "Ring Around the Rosey"
12 Hwy. aide
13 "But Not for Me" lyricist Gershwin
14 Took
15 What your answers to the capitalized clues should *not* be
17 IT COMES BEFORE FOUR
18 Gird (oneself)
19 Wielded
21 "Tower of ___" (thrill ride)
23 Thsi cleu hsa sveeral
26 Egg quantity
28 Actor Sizemore
29 IT COMES BEFORE FIVE
32 ___-eyed
33 IT COMES BEFORE SIX
34 Prefix with system
35 Crier's cry
37 After-tax amount
39 eBay figure
43 Bowling divisions
45 Early game maker
46 IT COMES BEFORE NINE
48 What your answers to the capitalized clues *should* result in
50 En ___
51 Start, as a program
52 "Gross!"
53 Big name in chips
54 "You bet!"
55 Gold standard: Abbr.

DOWN

1 Shakespearean word
2 Quickly fry
3 Circus worker, briefly
4 Hide out
5 Hockey legend
6 [It can't be!]
7 Have dreams
8 Use the wheel
9 Reason to dress up
10 Either Clinton, at one time
11 6–3, for one
16 Place
20 Some simple machines
22 Night flight
24 One of ten
25 Volume booster
27 Mauna ___
29 ___ party
30 Cooler must
31 Needed directions
33 Triangular letter
35 Oratorio composer
36 Longs
38 VCR button
40 Kind of eye surgery
41 Put up
42 They might pay off
44 Nimble
46 901, to Nero
47 Campus connection
49 Color

Good constructors don't care for it either, but such entries are handy because they're short and contain very common letters.

Doing enough puzzles to hammer these words into your head is key.

ANSWER, PAGE 92

THREE-WAY TIE

ACROSS

1 Wanted poster letters
4 Shakespearean foot
8 Arrival after an arm raise
11 Wood measure
13 Giant Procter & Gamble brand
14 Urban legend, maybe
15 Clue for 35-Across
17 Try
18 Elevator pioneer Otis
19 ___ panel
21 See 8-Down or 44-Across
22 DEA agents
24 Double-check
27 2 letters
30 See 29-Down or 44-Across
31 Lifters' spot
32 Maze setbacks
34 Logical, as an argument
35 See 15-Across or 44-Across
40 Double chin feature
42 Architectural support
43 ··· – – – ···
44 Phrase preceding 21-, 30-, or 35-Across
46 African creature
47 Geometry calculation
48 Great one?
49 Recipe qty.
50 Great ideas
51 What 10 may mean: Abbr.

DOWN

1 Took the stage
2 Australian critter
3 Adam or Alan in show biz
4 Hawkeye's home
5 Will Smith role
6 ___ best friend
7 Friends let them be 7-Down
8 Clue for 21-Across
9 Miles (from)
10 Word in some addresses
12 Going down: Abbr.
16 Ship pronoun
20 Word in many California cities
23 Class: Abbr.
24 Hr. division
25 Boolean connector
26 Metric measures: Abbr.
27 Modifier, maybe: Abbr.
28 Signal givers
29 Clue for 30-Across
30 Alarm
33 Pip place
35 Mel's Diner employee
36 Philosophers theorize about its meaning
37 Emcee's words
38 Work ___
39 One in a quire
41 Wasted no time
42 Palms, etc.
43 Certain NCO
45 Stipe's group, once

Want to get faster? Work on writing quickly!

In particular, don't put crossbars on your I's.

ANSWER, PAGE 92

ONE FOR THE EDITORS

ACROSS

1 Commute terminus, often
5 "The Big Bang Theory" network
8 Villain in "The Lion King"
12 "Typee" companion
13 Word with house or party
14 "Pass it to me!"
15 Good person to consult
16 Well thought-out
18 Tactic against a budget deficit
20 Soldiers, for short
21 Indian instruments
24 Video game item that may be accidentally thrown
28 Through
29 Bibliophile's prized item
33 14-Across, in France
34 Ladies' shirts
35 Seminoles' local rivals
39 Sticker
40 Italian food ingredient, maybe
45 Film in which Ralph Fiennes played Charles Van Doren
47 Ol' buddy
48 Unlikely to bite
49 Eisenhower, during his campaign
50 Bee or Em
51 Donna of classic TV
52 Place to retire
53 Change machine inserts

DOWN

1 Moving pieces
2 Annoyed response to an alarm
3 Moved like the dickens
4 "Bust a Move" rapper
5 Second half of a Texas city's name
6 "___ there" (sympathetic statement)
7 Wrenches in the gears
8 1985 Tears for Fears hit
9 Real fractions
10 Exist
11 Charity led by Bono
17 Poli ___
19 Christian of fashion
22 Really stinky
23 Goes, so to speak
24 Kristen of "SNL," once
25 Machu Picchu builder
26 "Are we going now?"
27 Go back
30 Committed a certain hockey infraction
31 Arrange fancily, as hair
32 Willemstad's island
36 Had a lot of, as confidence
37 Apt. count
38 Indian title
41 What pot holders do?
42 Keep away from
43 One might hum it
44 First responders, for short
45 Three mos.
46 Nation with red, green, white, and black in its flag

Some people also like to write E's like backwards 3's,

but I could never get used to that.

ANSWER, PAGE 92

APT ANAGRAM 4

ACROSS
1 Servant
5 Great composer
9 Be in the hole
12 Choir voice
13 Up to the task
14 Candy with a dispenser
15 Apt anagram of 50-Across
18 Basement
19 See 42-Across
20 "___ was saying ..."
21 Beer holder
22 Four performers
26 Indian royalty
30 Coffee holder
31 "Wicked!"
33 Self
34 ___ branch (symbol of peace)
37 Santa's runway
40 Naval rank: Abbr.
42 19-Across is part of it: Abbr.
43 There is ___ in numbers
46 Bets a lot, perhaps
50 Apt anagram of 15-Across
52 Epoch
53 Either host of an ESPN Radio show
54 Noted garden
55 Poker prize
56 Shoreline features
57 Written words

DOWN
1 ___ Antony
2 Lotion additive
3 "___ do" (expression of acceptance)
4 42-Across's currency
5 Roadblock
6 First three of 26
7 Loose garment
8 Therapist
9 Chooses, with "for"
10 168 hours
11 Poet Pound
16 Right on the map
17 Long story
22 Status ___
23 Internet acronym
24 "I'd like to buy ___" ("Wheel of Fortune" line)
25 Popeye, for one
27 Fast flier
28 "Long ___ and Far Away"
29 Emulate a kangaroo
32 Tennis game
35 Swerve
36 Bury
38 Scandinavian capital
39 Water flow controller
41 Damascus's country
43 Phase
44 Dynamic opening?
45 Brotherhood, for short
47 Lose color
48 Show off the muscles
49 Shipped
51 It's usually blue or gray

To pick up speed, try to read clues and

write other answers simultane-ously.

ANSWER, PAGE 92

CLOWNING AROUND

ACROSS

1 Guinness suffix
4 Tread the boards
7 Please, in Germany
12 Bard's however
13 Do a summer chore
14 What chariots do?
15 Start of a question
18 Very
19 Long race
20 Lean (on)
21 It can have a ball
23 Squeezing creature
26 It may be big
28 One with a famous belt
30 End of the question and start of its punny answer
34 Used a 3-Down on
35 Doesn't flow
36 Sucker
37 Surgeons' rooms
38 Gets to
42 Poultry
45 Tooth or animal
47 End of the answer
50 Eat right up
51 It often follows you
52 Pointy-eared creature
53 Inner plague
54 Say "I do"
55 Rd. crossers

DOWN

1 Old number?
2 Force forward
3 Bathroom item
4 Famous guy
5 Phoenix skaters
6 What a peace sign might indicate?
7 Get a sunburn
8 "Victory is mine!"
9 Try to intimidate an opponent, in a way
10 ___ Tuesday ('80s pop group)
11 H
16 Useful refrigerant
17 Certain Shoshone
22 Raring to go
24 "Gosh!"
25 Fire ___
27 Nothing spectacular
28 Globe
29 Like the sun in the east
30 Investing options, for short
31 Investing option, for short
32 Tear out of
33 Unlike the words in this crossword, I hope
37 "Yippee!"
39 Gets to
40 Prepared for a knighting
41 Lords' underlings
43 Not esto or eso
44 "What time?"
46 Got better, as wine
47 It will pass
48 A Grecian urn has one
49 It may drop

You have to be a little careful to ensure your letters are legible,

but the two actions don't have to be completely separate.

ANSWER, PAGE 92

THEMELESS CHALLENGE 2

ACROSS

1 Crazy
5 Dull color
9 Human genome project concern
12 Enthusiasm
13 First murderer
14 It's east of the Atl.
15 One way to graduate
18 Diversions
19 Some coding statements
20 "Twilight" heroine
22 Martin Crane's dog
24 "Wall-E" love interest
25 Ump's call
27 Wheel part
30 Handshaker, possibly
33 Long seat
34 Sea bird
35 &
36 Garbo on the screen
38 Sways
40 Face card
42 In the ___ (bad place to be left)
44 Step by step
48 Important stat: Abbr.
49 Nub
50 From the top
51 Work the land
52 Big name in stomach settlers
53 "It's a ___!"

DOWN

1 Real beauty
2 Menu words
3 Honkers
4 Yearly record
5 ___ homo
6 Something unsettling
7 A net loops through it
8 Solo
9 Contrived plot device
10 In the shower, say
11 Zeus's son
16 Gather
17 Former ABC show
20 Tries to get a treat, maybe
21 Liquid on a cooking show, briefly
23 Bruce or Laura
26 In ___ (upset)
28 Long and thin
29 Means justifiers
31 Challenged
32 Nero's land
37 Pass
39 Not quite an ennead
40 Hebrew letter
41 Golden rule preposition
43 Western Indians
45 "___ go, girl!"
46 Shook hands, perhaps
47 Grazer

In a tournament setting, one has to be quick without being hasty.

You might not have to read every clue,

ANSWER, PAGE 92

AFTER ONE TOO MANY ...

ACROSS

1 Accuse
7 Dieters in a rhyme
13 Tool used in the cold
14 Gray who was just a little too late to the patent office
15 ... the beekeeper was ___
16 ... the army commander was ___
17 Strong hold'em hole cards
19 Animal in Egyptian history
22 Dark force
23 Criterion, for short
27 ... the demolitionist was ___
30 Story's payoff, sometimes
31 Hectic place
32 Like some drinks
33 Ashley's the taller one
34 ... the linebacker was ___
35 MTV target
36 Everybody wants a piece of it
37 Not quite right: Abbr.
38 Throw out
42 ... the garbageman was ___
45 ... the fighter pilot was ___
49 Student's goal, frequently
50 Stare at, say
51 It may involve a wedge
52 Pointed style

DOWN

1 Harmless untruth
2 Hosp. area
3 ___ Percé (tribe)
4 ___ Strip
5 Suit
6 People often sleep on them
7 Take effect
8 Blueprint contents
9 Tolls loudly
10 Satisfy curiosity
11 It's sometimes ignored in alphabetization
12 Pathetic
18 Goof
19 Fancy neckwear
20 Parenthesis, possibly
21 Analyze in English class
24 It might be cash
25 Not left for leftovers
26 Partner in crime
28 Play part
29 Fourth-century brute
30 Hosp. scan
32 Run-down hotel
34 Recycle ___
36 Priest, informally
39 Heirs to the world, so it's said
40 ___ list
41 "Alex & ___" (2003 rom-com)
42 Used to be
43 One in a hill
44 Estonia or Lithuania, once: Abbr.
46 0 or 1
47 "Before" in only one syllable
48 Twisted Sister's Snider

but you should check a crossing if something looks weird.

It's a balance that comes with experience and practice.

ANSWER, PAGE 93

CRUNCH TIME

ACROSS

1 Some London hangouts
5 Urban problems
9 They may be part of 5-Across
12 Burn application
13 Red one?
14 Opposite of 34-Down
15 Unlike a wasteland
17 Inc., in England
18 Emulated Evel Knievel
19 Sharks' home
21 Boy Scout group
23 10, on a table
24 Before, at the beginning
27 Car that sounds like a bawl?
29 Mad ___
32 Workout tape, or this puzzle's theme when pronounced another way
36 Benin's neighbor
37 Cruise of "Rock of Ages"
38 Program in purl?
39 Campus marchers
42 Peacock network
44 Cheater, perhaps
47 Jazz segments
51 "Ol' buddy, ol' ___"
52 Word said before a disappearance
54 Chatroom query letters
55 Biggest of seven
56 Middle East flier
57 What 14-Across means
58 Lady's companion, for short
59 "La Bohème" derivative

DOWN

1 Like some vacations
2 Radius neighbor
3 Physicist Niels
4 Davy Jones's locker
5 "Gotta ___!"
6 Graceful riding horses
7 Italian fashion hub
8 It may be stolen
9 America had thirteen of them, originally
10 Adjoins
11 Fries, for one
16 Oft-abbreviated phrase
20 Put some life into
22 '60s arena, for short
24 Word with peeve or project
25 ___ Grande
26 Takeout orders, often
28 Slightly
30 Source of a famous 41-Down
31 202.5°
33 Cry from a wise one?
34 Opposite of 14-Across
35 Celestial shadow
40 It's steeped
41 See 30-Down
43 "The ___ House Rules"
44 Verb often uttered by Bob Barker
45 Knock down a peg
46 Reason for a delay
48 It ends with a moral
49 Drescher with a nasal voice
50 Wound worsener
53 ___ scan

Tournaments typically can't and don't score by the second,

so if you have time left in a scoring "window," use it!

ANSWER, PAGE 93

STRAIGHT FLUSHES

ACROSS

1 Day's beginning?
4 Like fan blades
9 Boxer's poke
12 Bachelor's last words
13 Bad thing to make in public
14 Caesar's breakfast?
15 Word in the Marines' slogan
16 Provisionary phrase
18 Superstar's avalanche
20 It's attractive
21 Fork part
22 Pried
25 "The BFG" author
27 Lady ___
30 Additionally
31 Got rid of
32 Genetic winder
33 Mercedes-___
34 Not gross
35 Speller's clarification
36 Face the day
37 Be a bad victor
39 Quote from a victor
41 Bank acct. gain
42 Words in a fish story
45 Reasons to be in bed
48 Announcer Hall
49 What's what, in Spain
50 Sedimentary rock
51 Hush-hush org.
52 Military fig.
53 Diamond covers
54 Opener

DOWN

1 Perturb
2 Light bulb, in comics
3 Bad place to go, or an alternate title for this puzzle
4 Like most people
5 American humorist/actor
6 Mend
7 Place to stay
8 Corrections are often made in it
9 Tom Joad's creator
10 Rd. relative
11 Kick out
17 Court
19 Like some salsa
23 Seemingly forever
24 Be bored, maybe
25 "Shoot!"
26 Rink leap
28 Tri- divided by three
29 "Need assistance?"
33 Super Mario ___
35 Bear witness (to)
38 Advice columnist Landers
40 Smartens (up to)
42 Former ruler
43 Romeo's last words
44 Aussie greeting
45 Information from some tests
46 Big guy
47 ___ Na Na

Make sure every square is filled and that your letters are at least somewhat legible.

You can also use the time to cross-check some clues that you may have skipped as you sped through.

ANSWER, PAGE 93

FROM THE MAILBAG

ACROSS
1 Pontiac classic
4 Dieter's nemeses
8 "Yo, sailor!"
12 Rower
13 Keep in touch, in a way
15 Positive feedback on my puzzles
17 Words to the Little Red Hen
18 Letters before a colon
19 It goes up and down
21 Tales of multiple adventures
26 Diamond's opposite, in hardness
29 Modest, as a skirt
30 Positive or negative feedback on my puzzles (it could go either way!)
35 Surfer's sobriquet
36 Arizona rival
37 Zany poet Nash
39 Make better
44 Letters between an 8 and a 0
47 Amos's friend
48 Negative feedback on my puzzles
53 Keep at it
54 It accompanies neither
55 Crichton menace
56 Sounds of scolding
57 Punk subgenre, popularly

DOWN
1 Graduates' wear
2 Western resort
3 Take the podium
4 Dept. of Health and Human Services div.
5 Cathedral sights
6 Horn sound
7 Find
8 The Greatest
9 Didn't seek
10 The ___ that got away
11 Word not heard from a nay-sayer
14 They're tall in Europe
16 Frank McCourt sequel
20 Had haggis, say
22 "Chasing ___"
23 Guy's partner
24 It fells things
25 Word often heard in boot camp
27 Brit's can
28 It's not often whole
30 Union announcement
31 Big ___ (affectionate words)
32 Math class term
33 Letter next to U, phonetically
34 X, sometimes
38 Film ___
40 Sidelines interjection
41 Not worth a second thought
42 Drive rapidly becoming obsolete
43 Prefix with plane
45 "Hey, you!"
46 Caesar's last words to Brutus
48 It goes boom
49 ___ majesty
50 "___ been better"
51 Health class subject
52 Photo finish?

Remember: This is supposed to be fun.

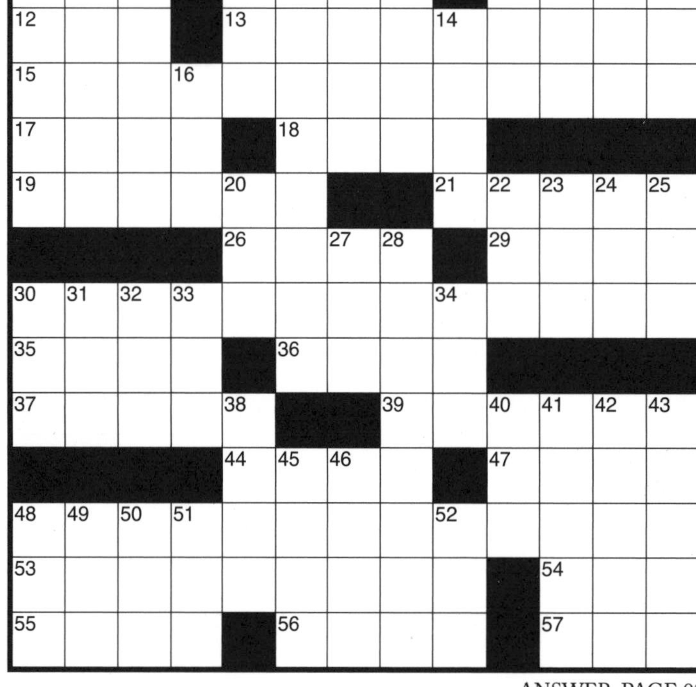

Don't get too hung up on frustrating

ANSWER, PAGE 93

MR. PUZZLE

ACROSS

1 Bit of advice
4 NYPD announcements
8 Party containers
12 Lennon's mate
13 Sirtis's sci-fi role
14 Forever
15 MISSED
18 Like some swimmers
19 In an unproductive manner
20 Be in a horde
21 Sicilian exploder
23 Praiseful lines
26 ___ doble (fast ballroom dance)
28 John Barth's "___ Goat-Boy"
30 MIST
34 "The game is ___!"
35 Lowly one
36 It ends in Nov.
37 ___ prof.
39 Old empire resident
43 Moppet of Mayberry
45 Toughen
47 MYST
50 ___ Xing
51 Prime creditors?: Abbr.
52 A pop
53 Bozo
54 One who just won't go away
55 One who can't pass the bar?

DOWN

1 Namely
2 Just plain silly
3 Wild West group
4 Abbr. before a name on an envelope
5 Think through
6 ___ Iver (folk band)
7 Audit a class
8 Friedrich's Communist collaborator
9 Albumen's complement
10 "I didn't know that!"
11 Grounded flier: Abbr.
16 One who can't get out of bed?
17 Slowly, in music
22 Big name in baseball cards
24 End's neighbor, for short
25 Suffix with Japan
27 Get
29 Diamond frame
30 Young chap
31 Conditions
32 Stopped worrying about
33 Stifles, as growth
38 Install, as a program
40 Some tides
41 Small role for a big actor
42 Red ___
44 Job attraction
46 Nifty
47 Pt. of speech
48 It passes, barely
49 Don't abstain

moments in your solving, whether it

pertains to speed or finishing.

ANSWER, PAGE 93

THEMELESS CHALLENGE 3

ACROSS

1 Estop
4 The winner breaks it
8 Whence to worship
12 Still exist
13 Last words?
14 Caramel candy
15 1995 electee
18 Re
19 Word often said while pointing
20 Dreaded one?
22 Varnish ingredient
25 Some calculators' features
27 Play divisions
29 Poet's inits.
30 Emulate Glenn
33 See 32-Down
34 What gets you stoned?
35 Pope called "the Great"
36 Corpulent
38 Large earthenware pots
40 Dramatist Chekhov
42 The end
45 Try to escape
48 It might be big
49 State, to 15-Across
50 Entertainment honors ceremony shown on Spike
51 Irish port
52 Nine-digit IDs
53 Superlative suffix

DOWN

1 ___ California
2 Muslim, often
3 Michael Phelps, e.g.
4 Shows off
5 Grandpa Simpson
6 Green snack
7 Use acid in art
8 Start a rebellion
9 Where chopping is frowned upon
10 ___ king
11 Mythical bird of enormous strength
16 Somewhat, to start
17 Mess (around)
21 "Cheerio!"
23 Part of an analogy
24 Radar O'Reilly's drink
25 Nutzoid
26 Whiner
28 Famed apple shooter
31 Angle's representation, frequently
32 Big name in 33-Across rental
37 ___ attack
39 Beds' places, sometimes
41 Miner's finds
43 Band's rent payers
44 Battle of Hoth combatant (and the reverse of 21-Down)
45 Tape recorder jack
46 Shakespeare's commotion
47 Indian bread

Don't neglect the theme.

You probably won't be able to solve a theme answer without at least a few letters,

ANSWER, PAGE 93

ON THE SLOPES

ACROSS

1 There are most often 51 or 54 per game
5 "The Andy Griffith Show" character
9 Good times
12 Extremely nitpicky
13 Fervor
14 Bust (on)
15 Ski very briefly?
18 Concession expression
19 Cut a rug
20 "Listen to me, sonny ..."
23 Aligned
24 "Cujo" author Stephen
26 Part of $E = mc^2$
27 Like a day spent skiing?
30 Job seeker, maybe
32 Actress Thompson
33 Didn't feel good
35 Chews out
40 Federline's ex
42 Not the sharpest knife in the drawer
43 "On my honor, I will ski"?
46 It's electric
47 Like the driven snow
48 Certain tournament
49 Turn red, maybe
50 Tommy Shaw's band
51 Team partly owned by Jay-Z

DOWN

1 Welcome sight in a desert
2 "I give up!"
3 Western lake and resort
4 Snowstorm aftermath
5 Lb. parts
6 ___ soup
7 Unstressed-stressed foot
8 1948 Nobel Prize for Literature winner
9 Montevideo's place
10 Gives spare change to, say
11 A bike might have ten
16 Plays sardines, possibly
17 ___ Jean (Marilyn Monroe's birth name)
21 Communion, e.g.
22 Bad guy
25 "It's only a ___"
27 Pubgoer's drink
28 Unimprovable
29 "Where's ___?"
30 Dissuaded, as rioters
31 Purveyor of the unbelievable
34 Is successful, as a putt
36 Unwise car buy
37 Shoot from afar
38 Ledger item
39 "Gossip Girl" viewers, probably
41 Most of the Internet, it seems
44 Get nosy
45 T. ___

but once you've figured out what's going on,

1	2	3	4	■	5	6	7	8	■	9	10	11
12				■	13				■	14		
15				16					17			
18					■	■	19					
20					21	22	■	23				
■	■	■	■	24			25	■	26			
■	■	27	28					29			■	■
30	31			■	32				■	■	■	■
33				34	■	35			36	37	38	39
40					41	■	■	42				
43						44	45					
46			■	47				■	48			
49			■	50				■	51			

you might be able to crack into a difficult corner by solving another theme answer.

ANSWER, PAGE 93

FOUR EASY PIECES

ACROSS

1 CFO's degree
4 Significant others, in chatroom lingo
7 Upside-down e
12 First coats
14 Teased, with "with"
15 "Did you see that?!?"
16 Monetary unit in Sri Lanka, Seychelles, Nepal, Mauritius, Pakistan, Maldives, or India
17 Ref's call
18 Some columns
19 Fire stirrer, after use
24 "Oh well ..."
25 Fish eggs, or a kind of deer
26 "Wanna ___?"
29 Shake up
30 Theme of this puzzle
32 ___-10 (acne medication)
33 Key used with numbers to type non-English characters
34 Modern art?
35 Drop the ball
36 Starchy side
40 Came up
42 Santa ___
43 Rights org.
44 It could win a horse race by a horn
48 Courtyards
49 It's called in
50 Showed to the foyer, say
51 One good at shooting people down
52 "... and more": Abbr.

DOWN

1 Radar gun's reading: Abbr.
2 Fraternity man, briefly
3 Feel feverish
4 Car insurance spokesanimal
5 ___ Loops
6 NNE's opposite
7 "Last Nite" band, with "the"
8 Two-doored vehicle
9 The graph y = ¹⁄x makes one
10 Some want it legalized
11 Gator tails?
13 They may be debunked
19 Indian prince
20 Israeli flier
21 An old one is riddled with holes
22 Asked too much
23 Alley-___
27 "No ___" (Sartre work)
28 If this clue has one, I'll be embarassed
30 Bakery holder
31 Charlemagne's realm: Abbr.
35 Play with, as Oreos
37 Medium of some art
38 ___ button
39 Tabled
40 Like a grammar Nazi
41 "At any ___ ..."
44 Frequent Olympics winner
45 Exultation in verse
46 Traitor
47 The Big Apple, for short

Have you ever seen a rebus crossword before?

In rebus puzzles, something other than a single letter

ANSWER, PAGE 93

HOP TO IT

ACROSS

1 The Concorde, e.g.
4 Long ones are risky
8 Rounds
12 "___ vadis?" (Latin for "Where are you going?")
13 "___ Trip" (Cuba Gooding Jr. film)
14 "That's pretty cool"
15 Remains holder
16 Bending the knees?
18 "... should that day come ..."
20 It may need oiling
21 Put at 000
22 Kind of shot
24 T, at times
25 Horse's father
26 Respite from bounding?
31 Is at war?
32 Wanted back
34 GI IDs
38 Waterproof boot
39 Register, in England
40 Where the chips are down
41 Use a time machine, maybe?
44 Uncle ___
45 Accomplish nothing
46 Created a web or a tale
47 NaOH, e.g.
48 Iditarod vehicle
49 Twitter message, e.g.
50 What you might shout if you finish this puzzle

DOWN

1 Peewee
2 Mozilla users
3 Pumps iron, say
4 ___ d'art
5 Not elated
6 Water gate
7 Engine additive
8 Con men?
9 Denoted
10 Character with blue hair
11 Web-footed swimmer
17 Blacksmith, at times
19 Don't drive straight
22 Silverman's portrayer
23 Eyes, in poetry
25 Secured
27 When in Rome, you're here
28 They end in -zoic
29 Good way to talk
30 What a good editor has
33 Their sole function is to mate
34 Some computers
35 Magic center, once
36 Barely nick
37 Overdrank
38 "___ that great?"
40 Heart
42 Winter setting in CT
43 Mimic

will appear in some squares.

There are a few in this book, so be on the lookout!

ANSWER, PAGE 93

EXCHANGE PROGRAM

ACROSS

1 "Hey, over here!"
6 Lie adjacent to
9 Smooth-tongued
12 "The March King"
13 Recyclable items
15 With 43-Across, the nature of the exchange
17 Sigma follower
18 Take a break, say
19 Sit or stay, possibly
20 Covering the most material
21 Sapporo swag
23 Feathers' surface
26 Morrison of music
30 The parties in the exchange
32 Like exams, sometimes
33 Get more Time
34 "Spring ahead" syst.
35 Stewart on "The Daily Show"
36 Sicilian sight
39 Florida ___
40 Goes back
43 See 15-Across
47 Like some deliveries
48 File folder stick-on
49 Singer Winehouse
50 Where to see C:\>
51 Best left alone

DOWN

1 Rice ___
2 State, or an Indian tribe native to it
3 Hawaiian shindig
4 Egyptian killer
5 Grabbing them is a no-no, in sports
6 Hearing aid?
7 Stooge Howard
8 Center's accumulation: Abbr.
9 Student's stat
10 Person for whose sake things are often done?
11 Gray
14 Like most arguments
16 "L.A. ___"
20 Big name in cars
21 "Sounds fine to me"
22 Outcome, redundantly
23 Formal crown
24 It may be chipped
25 Wall hangings
26 Deer meat
27 Luke, to Vader
28 See red?
29 Not quite straight up: Abbr.
31 6–4, say
35 President Bartlet on "The West Wing"
36 Make less difficult
37 Attention getter
38 Alluring
39 Boxer's stat
40 Punk subgenre
41 Track competition
42 Parisian suburb with an airport
44 Contribute
45 Big name in Communism
46 Sultry West

If you're looking for a greater sense of community in your puzzling,

check out the American Crossword Puzzle Tournament

ANSWER, PAGE 93

SIGN LANGUAGE

ACROSS

1 Nervous movement
4 Service station jobs
9 B'fast orders
12 Web scripting format designed to be human-readable
13 Saddam Hussein, for one
14 "Yeah, keep telling yourself that!"
15 Civil War battle, in the stars?
17 Simile middle
18 Jason of "My Name Is Earl"
19 Firearm accessory, in the stars?
21 More popular song, usually
23 Title role in a renowned film
24 Often-blamed look-alikes, in the stars?
29 Peaceful, in a sense
30 Take as spoils
31 "No ___" (Chinese menu phrase)
34 Seafood treat, in the stars?
36 He played Pierce
39 Old, say
40 Circus figure, in the stars?
45 What a performer takes
46 Toon who hates water
47 Kind of stockings, in the stars?
50 Day before
51 Wide
52 Org. with piece-ful rallies?
53 Cartoon character whose last name is Höek
54 Apt to be slapped
55 Web programming language

DOWN

1 Phone msg.
2 Cry after a close call
3 Tipped off
4 Lucy of "Kill Bill"
5 "Superman II" villainess
6 Roseanne's surname
7 Prefix similar to iso-
8 It may be hyperbolic
9 Butler's love
10 "FoxTrot" son
11 Comfortable spot in the summer
16 See stars
20 Take to the slopes
21 "___ who?"
22 Taj Mahal's locale
25 Bard's nightfall
26 Big ___
27 "___ been had!"
28 Less hurtful ball material
31 Singer whose middle name is Louise
32 Brochettes
33 Community college prereq, maybe
34 Frequently spelled word in preschool
35 They're summoned at airports
36 Make fit
37 Part of AWOL
38 Egg set
41 Police alerts
42 Actress Sorvino
43 Those, in Spain
44 Some electronic devices
48 Ice cream brand name
49 ___ water

You'll find warm, welcoming people who love puzzles!

and the National Puzzlers' League.

ANSWER, PAGE 93

THEMELESS CHALLENGE 4

ACROSS

1 Pizarro's victim
5 ___ Minor
9 Prez with dogs named Him and Her
12 First and third quarter tide
13 Creator of linking rings?
14 Valuable underground find
15 "You're welcome"
18 Pong purveyor
19 Cheep trill
20 "Return of the Jedi" location
22 Tough tests
24 Agnus ___ (Christian emblem)
25 "Take ___"
27 It explodes in Sicily
30 It might not be for the faint of heart
33 Seymour's one-time Springfield Elementary love
34 It may be burned
35 Big name in electronics
36 Bathroom oddity
38 Famous twin name
40 Brand name with a "long vowel" symbol in its logo
42 ___ of Langerhans (pancreas part)
44 1965 epic
48 It's often about nothing
49 Perlman of "Cheers"
50 Place for princely pedagogy
51 Desire
52 Noted accomplishment?
53 Change the decor of

DOWN

1 Neither Rep. nor Dem.
2 "The One," in "The Matrix"
3 1995 comedy about a North American cold war
4 Is ___ (probably will)
5 Declare as true
6 One who gets discounts
7 Bank accrual: Abbr.
8 ___ Bath (prank call name)
9 Nickname derived from a flag
10 Cheese plate choice
11 Leader of the Blackhearts
16 Popular parade month?
17 Tiny hooter
20 Risky place
21 RPI student, stereotypically
23 1990 baseball champs
26 Cabinet member
28 French resort
29 Codebreaker Turing
31 Brush up?
32 Its full name starts with Escherichia
37 1991 Oliver Stone film, with "The"
39 Seesaw, for instance
40 1940s climax
41 Pestered persistently
43 Thick carpet
45 P
46 Mercury or Venus
47 Plastic ___ Band

Has the crossword construction bug bitten you?

The website called Cruciverb has great information,

ANSWER, PAGE 93

SPIT IT OUT

ACROSS

1 Respond, on "Jeopardy!"
4 Range of frequencies
8 Big gulp
12 Where the Gobi is
14 Actor's "I forgot"
15 B-ball?
17 First filing cabinet's label, maybe
18 Toucan on a cereal box
19 Widely used chatting program
22 Center
26 Part of an executive ensemble
31 The world's longest flower?
32 C-clamp?
34 Suffix with million
35 Dragon slayer of English lore
36 "Pinball wizard"
38 Hither's partner
39 "Ich bin ___ Berliner"
41 Blimpie offerings
45 D-day?
51 Contribute, as to a message board
52 The public
53 X, Y, and Z, but not W
54 Sparrow's portrayer
55 Move in a curvy path, say

DOWN

1 Big bowling equipment mfr.
2 Couch
3 Masseuse's aim
4 Pelt relentlessly
5 In the style of
6 0
7 Mentors, possibly
8 Hit really hard
9 Get the highest, or maybe the lowest, score
10 Ltd. equivalent
11 "That's quite interesting"
13 Miracle-___ (garden brand)
16 Hoover, e.g.
20 "Correct"
21 Like gum, often
23 Big name in fashion
24 Get through mud
25 Prefix with marketing
26 Dope
27 State that's round at both ends?
28 Early bird's victim
29 They appear periodically
30 Item for the toaster
33 Anticipate pain, maybe
37 Feminine side
40 Big city heroes: Abbr.
42 It often contains slashes
43 Judge's liability
44 Punch
45 Relaxing locale
46 Tortured franchise, until 2004
47 Application
48 Master of the macabre
49 Very, very softly, on a staff
50 Opus ___ (religious group featured in "The Da Vinci Code")

including a forum for asking questions

and, if you like, finding a mentor.

ANSWER, PAGE 94

WHY BOTHER?

ACROSS

1 Match parts
5 "Hell!" in Hamburg
8 Not completely closed
12 What may be used to build a castle?
13 Nomar's wife
14 Place to stay in Pamplona
15 It's pointless
18 Knowledgeable about
19 Make half-and-half?
20 Gets four balls
22 Peat ___
23 Opinion
24 Lendl of tennis
25 Removes bugs from
27 It's pointless
32 They're rented for big nights
33 Big hairstyles, for short
34 Open water
37 Getting shorter, as a candle
38 Devoured
39 For nothing
41 Geometry calculation
42 It's pointless
46 Witticism
47 Good name for a litigious woman?
48 Forearm part
49 De-squeaks
50 Yanks' foes
51 Be undecided

DOWN

1 Lotion figure
2 ___ de cologne
3 In name only
4 "Wait and Bleed" band, whose members wear masks
5 Prayer ending
6 Secretive org.
7 Bowlers' holders
8 Pocket ___ (fortuitous Texas hold'em dealing)
9 Outlaw Jesse
10 Dog watchdogs: Abbr.
11 Frayed and worn, as clothes
16 Article in El País
17 Hobbes, for one
20 "Ease on Down the Road" musical, with "The"
21 Blvd. relative
22 "Carmen" composer
25 Sexy or shrewd quality
26 Become less strict
28 Member of the lily family
29 Excessively sweet and sentimental stuff
30 Marker from the shy
31 Sixth sense: Abbr.
34 He sang the praises of thongs
35 Ho-hum feeling
36 To no ___ (pointlessly)
38 "___ you really?"
40 iPad purchases
41 Peak
43 The Dynamic ___
44 Where to get a room
45 Sonny

If you're in a competitive setting,

don't bother crossing out the clues (or the clue numbers)

ANSWER, PAGE 94

DOOR PRIZES

ACROSS

1 Has the power
4 Article with 1-Down
7 626 creator
12 GI entertainers
13 First name in comic book villainy
14 Prestigious institutions
15 Short reading
17 It can be used as a trumpet
18 Magician's show-stopper?
20 Slide stones on ice
21 Reel's partner
22 Slavic person
24 Actress Aniston, in the tabloids
25 Mud bath's place
28 Inquiry about candy?
32 "Not ___"
33 What O might mean, in a letter
34 Lit sign
35 Luau-welcoming present
36 Travel through time, say
38 Choice being unconventionally exercised in this puzzle
43 2008 Summer Olympics host
44 Griffith on the silver screen
45 Put off
46 Codebreaking org.
47 Fox alternative
48 Tournament favorites
49 "___ alive!"
50 Prob. take-off hour

DOWN

1 See 4-Across
2 Yesterday, say: Abbr.
3 Widely known
4 Bush ally
5 Kingly
6 Lutz relative
7 Teeny tiny units
8 Don't embrace
9 30, on a table
10 Where to find kings and queens
11 Fireplace "crumb"
16 ___ gear
19 Computer programming structure
22 Dormitory, maybe, to a parent
23 Bard's before
24 Wine holder
25 It was last minted in 1970
26 Luau food
27 Child's first pet, maybe
29 Ric Ocasek's band
30 Ovaltine rival, once
31 Word before cotta or firma
35 Like writing paper
36 Obtain with a struggle
37 Country album?
38 "Get ___ to a nunnery" ("Hamlet" quote)
39 Crawling (with)
40 Potent start?
41 Isn't wrong?
42 Be inclined (to)
43 Jukebox contents

that you've already solved.

It's a big time-waster.

ANSWER, PAGE 94

NOT A SINGLE WORD

ACROSS

1 Musical genre
4 Seafood choice
8 Vijay Singh's homeland
12 Become an expatriate
14 Soon, in a 53-Across
15 Single branch of a student loan office?
16 Science students' headaches
17 Inconvenient time for a phone call, probably
18 Animation collectibles
20 Single strand of pasta?
25 ___ kick (pool maneuver)
28 Lose it
29 People often disagree about what it is
30 Cut (off)
32 AAA offering
33 "Have a look at that!"
36 Gets sicker
39 Single singer without instruments?
41 ___ word (word incorporated into one language from another)
42 Sailor's delight
46 Dancer's control
48 Single West Indies island?
51 Jack Black/Ben Stiller bomb
52 Anybody's game
53 To make this clue fun / I've written this one
54 Primetime sitcom rating, possibly
55 "That was Zen, this is ___!" (punny punchline)

DOWN

1 Mexican capital
2 Where a Muscat-eer is from?
3 Not a neat stack
4 Curls tightly
5 Charlotte of "The Facts of Life"
6 24-hour bread source: Abbr.
7 Summer destination
8 Get beaten by
9 Perturbed
10 Tested person, in the Bible
11 Connections
13 Composition of an eye, maybe
19 Brain wave monitor: Abbr.
21 Name in a 2001 merger
22 Dog's warning
23 Knowing a lot about
24 Plies a needle
25 It covers a lot of time
26 Gator's relative
27 Shout from Dr. Frankenstein
31 Washington worker, briefly
34 Leotard, for one
35 It cares for the air: Abbr.
37 Court climax
38 Salmonlike fish
40 Make into law
43 Buckets
44 Plastic in a wallet, maybe
45 Gas station name in Canada
46 Workout unit
47 Musician Brian
49 Election mo.
50 Dough left on the table

Finally breaking through on your own

on a tough puzzle can be extremely satisfying,

ANSWER, PAGE 94

SEE HERE

ACROSS

1 ASAP, more informally
4 ___ Constitution
7 Suit
12 One on a board
14 Boxer's arm statistic
15 See 34-Across
16 Funnyman Lange
17 Alan of "M*A*S*H"
18 Buggers?: Abbr.
19 Summer drink often spelled with a "d"
22 See 41-Down
25 Essay length unit
26 Diamondback or Cub, e.g.
28 Will Smith film
29 Director Lee
30 Explosive times in the stock market
31 Saying "number" after it is redundant
32 Have a bawl?
33 Suffix with disk
34 Chess target
35 See 11-Down
37 Tour de France units
39 Shock's partner
40 The Miners of the NCAA
41 Fills to the brim
43 See 25-Across
47 A red one is major
48 Address for a manly man
49 Gets bent out of shape
50 Nimrod
51 Its symbol is derived from "stannum"

DOWN

1 What TDs and FGs get you
2 "Forgot About ___" (Eminem song)
3 "Come again?" in Cádiz
4 Useful
5 Briefly communicate
6 Genesis source
7 Pick-me-ups
8 Suitable for Halloween
9 Gluttonous, say
10 This place, in France
11 Starting word, often
13 Word with ice or figure
19 "No bid"
20 Paddled craft
21 Helicopter, slangily
22 Most college students go through eight
23 Skirt style with a flared bottom
24 Food for the football game, maybe
27 Destiny
30 Biddings
34 Greek letter
36 Annoyance
38 Forms a crowd
40 West Point inst.
41 Frightfest with many sequels
42 Imitating
44 Series of scenes
45 Trigram associated with 4
46 Time spent in the waiting room, it seems

but it's okay to give up if you're no longer having fun.

Look up the answers online or in the answer section so you can learn and improve.

ANSWER, PAGE 94

THEMELESS CHALLENGE 5

ACROSS

1 Rapper ___ Jon
4 Button hit when the phone rings, maybe
8 Hardly eye-popping
12 "Take On Me" band
13 Work site inspectors: Abbr.
14 100 cents
15 Number scrolling at the bottom of the screen, maybe
18 Prepare, as data for printing
19 Misrepresent
20 Be a troll, say
22 City with famous steaks
25 Fashionable tea
27 Cereal staple
29 Took the pot
30 Obsess over former glories
33 "Well fought!"
34 Bad news at NASA
35 Barely scrapes (out)
36 Classical Greek order
38 Give an address
40 Entertain, in a way
42 Drinker's spree
45 Sport featuring two blades per person
48 Anticipatory days
49 On your ___ (alert)
50 Unlikely Triple Crown winner
51 Piquancy
52 Name of two of Henry VIII's wives
53 Pontiac classic

DOWN

1 Chaps
2 Their goods are stacked
3 Probabilistic principle
4 Bread or lettuce
5 Armed Forces branch: Abbr.
6 "Things haven't changed"
7 Freedom from problems
8 Casual fabric
9 Upset loss, say
10 Exist
11 Try to knock out
16 2000 Best Supporting Actress
17 White flag words
21 Not stereo
23 Get wet, with "down"
24 Farm dwellers that don't grow anything
25 Putz
26 Town on the Big Island
28 Hammer holder
31 Receive, as a penalty
32 ___ four
37 "It's beyond my control"
39 Take down a peg
41 ___ trap
43 Camping pest
44 Breakfast brand with a rhyming slogan
45 "That '70s Show" character
46 "(___ Had) the Time of My Life"
47 "Jeopardy!" giant Jennings

On rare occasions, puzzlemakers will disguise clues

by using common clue phrases differently.

ANSWER, PAGE 94

3×4

ACROSS

1 Where to grab a cup of joe
5 Web language developed by Microsoft
8 Infant's wear
11 They might come from taps
12 Comedienne Margaret
13 Dot follower, on campus
14 Ill-suited to
17 "America's Got Talent" judge Howard
18 Twist it and dunk it
19 Poetic praise
21 Pretentious
25 Rude question, maybe
29 The Almighty
30 Make shorter
31 Not ital.
32 Cantonese dish of chicken and vegetables
37 The shortest one loses
38 Big inits. in fashion
39 Enthusiasm
42 Soup scooper
46 Nickname for Willie Mays
49 It's over a tennis player's head
50 Place for a mud bath
51 Green affliction?
52 Big cheese, for short
53 Ball ___ (one who is not a team 36-Down)
54 Bread ingredients

DOWN

1 Gives the sack
2 Often
3 Big party
4 Third-party holding
5 Performance
6 "Begone with you!"
7 Cause flooding, say
8 Not following
9 "___ declare!"
10 It might stick to your sock
15 Annul
16 What's jerked at the movies?
20 Tickled creature
22 "America's Next Top Model" host Banks
23 "Just be patient"
24 "Delectable!"
25 "Give a ___ ..."
26 Spray's target, maybe
27 Hound (as either a noun or a verb)
28 ___ message (something to set when you go on vacation)
29 Baseball bigwigs: Abbr.
33 Open structure
34 Has a gambling problem, perhaps
35 Land in the water?
36 One in the game
40 Pageant wear
41 Copy editor's catch
43 Big inits. in fashion
44 Like some TV
45 Ben & Jerry's rival
46 "No Scrubs" group
47 Shed item
48 Old witch

[Sample, for example] might clue RHYME

while [Ancients, for instance] hints at ANAGRAM.

ANSWER, PAGE 94

O MY!

ACROSS

1 "___ Diesel" (rap album by an NBA star)
5 Pirate's take
9 Promgoer's nightmare
12 Wise leader
13 2004 electoral battleground
14 Kimono sash
15 Stun
18 "Lemme ___!"
19 Promgoers' rides
20 Davy or Casey
22 He was assassinated in Mexico
24 8, in a date: Abbr.
25 What a bather's finger might resemble
26 Pin site
32 They're licked in hunger
33 Role for Keanu
34 Colons, turned 90°
37 "SNL" rival
39 Poker possibilities
40 New York city that's home to Rensselaer Polytechnic Institute
41 Stoplight alternative
46 "In Between Now and Then" band
47 Graceful horse named for where it comes from
48 Follow persistently
49 Quart divs.
50 Bank (on)
51 Sciences' counterpart

DOWN

1 Army NCO
2 "Can you run that by me again?"
3 Adapt, as a musical composition
4 Bartlett's entry
5 Easily broken
6 First baseman, in a classic sketch
7 Let out, as grievances
8 Cooperate
9 What a rocket does
10 Apple product, once
11 Having downed a few
16 Badgers' home: Abbr.
17 1.76 pints
20 It drops in surprise
21 "Not in ___ house!"
22 Stumbles
23 Plate crossings
25 Conspire
27 Wolf (down)
28 To this point
29 Brickyard racer
30 A birdie might hit it
31 www.cia.___
34 "Gimme five!"
35 Tennis player Safin
36 False witnesses
37 Diagnostic scan: Abbr.
38 Left ventricle attachment
40 Frozen treat chain, familiarly
42 Angry attitude
43 ___ Ripken Jr.
44 Drunk
45 Rival of Singh and Woods

It's good to have the right writing utensil,

particularly if you're in a tournament setting.

ANSWER, PAGE 94

NOT QUITE

ACROSS

1 It gives resorts on companies: Abbr.
4 Sedate leaders: Abbr.
7 Cartoon doc
12 Jeff Lynne's bane
13 Dadaist Sean
14 Shark weapon
15 Hoffman firm
17 Expended attack
18 All of these have a type
20 Dries, with "the"
21 It might start with WOW
22 With 35-Across, mate this puzzle salutes
25 Try to sin
29 Pry for
30 Chinese man
31 Org. that can top your car
32 Family audition
35 Set 22-Across
37 Boar implement
38 Stinky stuff
39 All of them have a type
44 Comedian Ellen
46 Dale, by birth
47 Actress Kerry
48 She's shaved for wood
49 Place for a mud bash
50 Playful sex critter
51 Farmer geog. unit
52 Reading winds, say

DOWN

1 Wagers
2 Suck, paradoxically
3 It's slammed in anger
4 School in Poughkeepsie
5 Goody-goody
6 Went too fast
7 Take for granted
8 They might involve oil
9 High schooler
10 Floor covering
11 The loneliest number
16 Pro-British one, in colonial times
19 Fisherman's device
22 "Honest" one
23 Get to second base, say
24 Change colors
25 Heavy weight
26 IRS collection
27 Science experiment locale
28 One might lend it
30 Ear pieces?
33 Idle drawing
34 Representation
35 Cry during a race, maybe
36 Larry of baseball
38 Little pests
39 Ken, for one
40 Humans' ancestors
41 Fashion magazine
42 Fixated
43 Response to a proposition, maybe
44 Try to seduce
45 Clumsy person

I like a mechanical pencil with .9mm lead, which doesn't break on me.

I also like having a big eraser that can be twisted up and down.

ANSWER, PAGE 94

THEMELESS CHALLENGE 6

ACROSS

1 Makes more romantic, as lights
5 It comes before boy or girl
9 Oft-married celeb, in tabloids
12 Irish New Age singer
13 Gridiron progress
14 Half of eleven?
15 Olsen twins bomb of 2004
18 Navel type
19 Sweats a lot, say
20 "What can Brown ___ you?"
22 Pass on, as a video
24 Diamonds, in slang
25 "Holy moly!"
27 Breeze (through)
30 Actor's asset
33 The Nutmeg State: Abbr.
34 Pie's place, perhaps
35 Pester persistently
36 Karate schools
38 Lets customers in
40 "I'm an expert!"
42 Word before limits or space
44 Director's shout
48 "Hänsel ___ Gretel"
49 Part of a Confederate signature
50 Letterhead feature
51 Total idiot
52 Asian scare
53 Bad reception effect

DOWN

1 Iniquity's locale?
2 Like Beethoven's Seventh
3 Wayans sitcom that ran from 2001 to 2005
4 Issue a rejection
5 Prefix with culture
6 Captures
7 Tiny one
8 Singer Baker or Bryant
9 Former "Family Feud" host
10 Like many airports: Abbr.
11 Puzzle features?
16 Deli specification
17 Like Odin
20 Compact ___
21 Eight at the beginning
23 Tar ___
26 ___ facto
28 Shortcut's representation
29 Staying power
31 Travelocity mascot
32 Sinful animal?
37 Ballet jumps
39 What sunburned skin does
40 "Barbie Girl" band
41 Phoenix hoopsters
43 Cougars' rivals
45 Schnozz end?
46 ___ trip
47 Penalty for prohibited parking

In a tournament setting, some crosswords

can be more trying simply because of their big size.

ANSWER, PAGE 94

COLLEGE YRS.

ACROSS
1 It's not true
5 Ness, for one
9 The Mannings, e.g.
12 Worksite inspectors: Abbr.
13 Aahs' partners
14 Oman's neighbor: Abbr.
15 FR.
17 Denominator of every whole number
18 Backpack securers
19 Slightly
20 SO
23 Beatle bride
24 Where to enter this answer?
25 Beer serving
29 Hive substance
33 Mystical field
35 Needing an upgrade
36 J.R.
42 Scribbles (down)
43 "Tough"
44 Golfer from South Africa
45 SR.
48 Money manager: Abbr.
49 Rant and rave, say
50 Have rolling in the aisles
51 "For shame!"
52 Team that famously had an 18–1 record, for short
53 Shady group?

DOWN
1 Soft shoe, for short
2 Fashion inits.
3 What a drink might hit
4 Bret who wrote about Poker Flat
5 Like dogs, they say
6 Polka band sound
7 Purify
8 QVC alternative
9 Interviewer's tidbit
10 Snooze-inducing
11 Not well-maintained
16 Cur's warning
19 With, north of the border
20 Break down
21 Game with Wild cards
22 Rage
26 Lies on the sand, perhaps
27 Big galoot
28 It gained independence from Ethiopia in 1993
30 Wrote a juicy autobiography, say
31 One of the eight states bordering Tenn.
32 Map lines: Abbr.
34 Consecrate, in a way
36 Pilot's emergency button
37 Gobbles (down)
38 "No need for apologies"
39 Taboos
40 Crunched items
41 Memory stumble
45 Leading scorer, maybe
46 "That's me"
47 Nelson Rockefeller was its gov.

It can be difficult to maintain your initial speed throughout your solving.

Practice on larger puzzles to build your endurance.

ANSWER, PAGE 94

ROUND TRIP

ACROSS

1 "Meatballs" character
5 Airline reservation
9 Inits. of a general and president
12 What Joseph Ratzinger became
13 Foot part
14 Oedipus, for one
15 In the clear, after a single?
17 Fender attachment
18 Big ___
19 Myopic Mr.
21 Is influential
24 Studio sign
26 "Come on, be a ___"
27 Medicine, after a stolen base?
31 Scandinavian capital
33 Suit at the top of a ladder
34 Teen's bane
35 Used, after a wild pitch?
38 Time to remember
39 The Last ___ (Bethany, in "Dogma")
40 Done, as bread
42 Earth bound?
44 Boxer's blow
45 Attraction in San Diego or the Bronx
46 Underdeveloped countries, after a suicide squeeze?
52 Auditing org.
53 Fix, as typos
54 Browns' state
55 Teen's bane
56 Men play up to five
57 LeBron rival

DOWN

1 Beachgoer's stat
2 Hawaiian treat
3 Big month for the 52-Across
4 Having a kick
5 Not out
6 Be human?
7 Courier's coup
8 Stick it to ___
9 They're over very quickly
10 Free download, perhaps
11 Nat, once
16 Word after ring or coin
20 Verdi opera set in Egypt
21 Find
22 Laundry
23 Hysterical cry
24 It has a floor
25 When both hands are up?
28 Unfurnished house's feature
29 Concerning
30 Campus bigwig
32 Killer whale
36 Postprandial chore
37 Shootout shout
41 Mac derivative
42 Tariq of Iraq
43 Singer Amos
44 Giant rivals
47 Poet's praise
48 Cambridge sch.
49 Letter before sigma
50 Women's ___
51 Buck's mate

Improving your mental abilities in general

can help you solve puzzles better.

ANSWER, PAGE 94

UNBALANCED DIET

ACROSS

1 Lead-in to boy or girl
5 Agnus ___
8 Resort locale, maybe
12 Semester
13 Hold the deed to
14 First murderer
15 Brockovich portrayed by Julia Roberts
16 Humiliated
18 RNSEGE
20 Ingredient in some milk
21 Still in it
24 Awoken
27 Part of EU: Abbr.
28 "From my cold dead hands" org.
29 GESG
32 Macabre writer
33 Consonant-free assent
34 Loosens or lightens
35 ___ report
37 Not conjugated normally, as a vb.
38 LASDA
43 Eau source?
45 Give up
46 Runner's goal
47 SOs might follow them
48 Humiliate, in a way
49 Editorial mark
50 Place
51 Barely got, with "out"

DOWN

1 "Up and ___!"
2 Hatcher of "Desperate Housewives"
3 It's not rabbit food
4 Frequent soap opera plot device
5 Suspicious
6 Water carrier
7 Young actress, perhaps
8 "Sorry, prior engagement"
9 Tunes about troubles
10 "Let sleeping dogs ___"
11 Maze marking
17 Asks for again
19 Teapot dweller of kiddie lit
22 Lust, for one
23 Itar-___ (Russian news agency founded in 1902)
24 Cleopatra's killer and kin
25 Tartan wearer
26 Big paper
27 Peyton's little brother
30 Where to get picked up
31 Loud music's upshot
36 Available, as an apartment
37 Common abbreviation, in full form
39 Start of a line that ends "Then fall, Caesar!"
40 Raft's undoing
41 Wood shaper
42 One in a Monopoly stack
43 Former TV home of the Braves
44 Meal portion?

ANSWER, PAGE 95

SWEET!

ACROSS

1 Nearly
6 "Goody Two Shoes" singer
13 "Tiny Bubbles" singer
14 Biblical barber?
15 CRUNCH
17 "The Book of ___" (Denzel Washington film)
18 Smash's opposite
19 French restaurant freebie
20 Stage fright
22 MARS
25 Played Pictionary, say
26 Boris's evil partner
27 Alternate title for this puzzle?
30 Contract pieces
33 ___ California
37 SNICKERS
38 Flock's leader
40 "___ Your Thing" (Isley Brothers song)
41 Sit-up targets
42 Forensic science series
43 MOUNDS
48 Half a quart
49 Supermarket path
50 They're hardly celebrities
51 Doles (out)

DOWN

1 Something next to a +
2 Steam generator part
3 Winning and winning and winning
4 "Weird Al" Yankovic film
5 Sheer fabric
6 Syllables after "rub"
7 Keyboard key
8 Keyboard key
9 Caltech rival
10 1986 James Cameron sequel
11 Man who made a famous guarantee
12 Our nation
16 Reciprocal of sec
21 Classic car that stopped production in 2003
22 Uncle Sam's take
23 Words before loss or disadvantage
24 Two-syllable units
26 Video game lover's treasure
28 Smoker's debris
29 Legal word before "judicata" or "publica"
30 Tie that some find tasteless
31 Barrio resident
32 "Pride and Prejudice" author
34 Profitless way to sell things
35 Bump and elbow
36 Emerges, as a situation
38 It's supported by "viewers like you"
39 Northeast Indian state
41 Sciences' partner
44 22-Down expert: Abbr.
45 That guy
46 Almost right, direction-wise: Abbr.
47 Competitive eaters' dish, frequently

Don't feel like your speed-solving has to flow seamlessly

from the upper left corner to the bottom right.

ANSWER, PAGE 95

KNOW THE RULES

ACROSS

1 First ___
4 Quiznos offerings
8 Thrown for a ___
12 Queensland borders it
14 Better Than ___
15 Rule introduced by the NHL in 2005: They're allowed!
17 Flavorful
18 Frequent documentary shower
19 eBay actions
22 Go off, as an alarm
25 Rule #2: After icing violations ...
30 Genre some find whiny
31 Miss Piggy, to herself
32 Clay, after converting
33 Rule #3: This will lead to fewer whistles!
38 Where to put a pat
39 Starts' partner
40 Big moneymaker
42 Sonic the Hedgehog's treasure
46 Rule #4: If it's still tied after overtime ...
51 Reason to open a window
52 Start rashly
53 Jobs for AAA
54 Picks, with "for"
55 Oft-debunked ability

DOWN

1 Plays a role
2 Only state whose postal abbeviation is two vowels
3 Lemon ___
4 Scored a run, maybe
5 Mil. branch
6 Geography or spelling event
7 Intimidating NFLer Warren
8 Ease
9 Lb. divisions
10 Mined find
11 Faux ___
13 It gets you off the hook
16 "Mamma Mia!" band
20 Aspiring musician's tape
21 "So what?" for example
23 "Heavens above!"
24 Scorer of 1,281 goals
25 Target for 24-Down
26 Actor Sharif or Epps
27 The Playboy bunny, for one
28 "If I had a ___" (palindrome)
29 Bro's counterpart
34 Stress upshots, sometimes
35 It may be guilty
36 Sharpeners
37 Question in Matthew 26
41 Fjord setting
43 What one little piggy had
44 Old Nickelodeon show with the Aggro Crag
45 Red's meaning, often
46 On a winning streak
47 Shakespeare wrote about much of it
48 "I do" is one
49 With it, decades ago
50 Granola morsel

Of course, having letters from crossing entries improves your chances of solving a clue,

but don't be shy about moving to a different section if you run into some difficulty.

ANSWER, PAGE 95

THEMELESS CHALLENGE 7

ACROSS

1 Inexperienced
4 Knight backers
8 ICQ receptions: Abbr.
12 Mediterranean, e.g.: Abbr.
13 Personal: Prefix
14 Milk-giving animals
15 Attractive, many would say
18 Assign
19 "Sexy" Beatles girl
20 Ring in a throwing game
22 Rowdy ___ (Clint Eastwood's role in "Rawhide")
25 Keep away from
27 Like some thermometers
29 Middle East org.
30 Comment after a corporate snafu
33 Firefox input
34 Word after duct or masking
35 Just ___
36 Balearic Islands resort
38 Person in the background
40 Parties
42 Impose a 38-Across duty on, and an anagram of 38-Across
45 1957 Elvis film
48 Like fine cheese and wine
49 Tricky ___ (Nixon nickname)
50 Afore
51 Talk like this he does
52 Up-and-down business?
53 Palindromic song by a palindromic band

DOWN

1 Working there *is* rocket science
2 Robbie's daredevil dad
3 Hirable
4 Prefix with -graph
5 Response to a minister
6 Men's Wearhouse purchase
7 Place to crash
8 Press conference throng
9 Thanksgiving treats
10 ___-X
11 Quick way across the pond, once: Abbr.
16 Establish
17 Peaceful poem
21 Caucus setting
23 "___ Minnow Pea" (wordplay-filled novel)
24 "You've got a deal!"
25 Feng ___
26 Sage, for one
28 Pat : "Wheel of Fortune" :: ___ : "Jeopardy!"
31 Pot supply
32 Cooked less
37 Nintendo princess
39 Hardly easy trips
41 ___ list
43 Prefix for height
44 Vintage Jaguar models
45 Homer Simpson's middle name
46 A while ___
47 Comp. ___

The wide-open spaces in

a themeless puzzle can be very daunting.

ANSWER, PAGE 95

ONE FROM THE ARCHIVES

ACROSS

1 Wooed successfully
4 Underhanded
7 Poolside marking
12 Caesar's salad ingredients?
13 Half a laugh
14 The Donald's second ex
15 "Bon appétit, everyone!"
17 Summaries' contents
18 Sessions with a famous psychologist?
20 Imitate
21 Presently
24 "Good buddy"
27 Rearward
28 Mr. Nahasapeemapetilon of "The Simpsons"
29 Some wins for a certain soccer star?
33 It can be worth one or eleven
34 "Yadda yadda yadda": Abbr.
35 They may be pale
36 Place for worshipers
38 Wallach of "The Magnificent Seven"
40 Some adaptations of macabre stories?
45 "Peace!"
47 She played Ferris Bueller's girlfriend
48 "Beats me"
49 Device that a TiVo often replaces
50 Cartoonist's collectible
51 Delivery specialist?
52 With 53-Across, comment often heard in the summer
53 See 52-Across

DOWN

1 ___ whistle
2 Past, emotionally
3 Cold War force
4 Oft-forgotten Stooge
5 Sailor's time off
6 Bigfoot's relative
7 Start, as a meal
8 1996 role for Madonna
9 Course option
10 It goes boom
11 Holds
16 False flattery
19 Prepare flour, maybe
22 Saber kin
23 Unlikely fighter
24 Chuck's alternative nickname
25 One of the Three B's
26 Coming out
27 Major ath. conference
30 Deer meat
31 Express lane unit
32 Searches for food, drugs, or panties
37 Twists
38 Render homeless
39 Bad witnesses
41 The year I made this puzzle (it's hidden in the three longest answers)
42 "To ___ his own"
43 Treat that twists
44 It's thrown superstitiously
45 It's often about nothing
46 Name

Getting a few shorter entries first may help you

break into a few longer ones, sending you well on your way to completion.

ANSWER, PAGE 95

ONE FOR THE AGES

ACROSS
1 Malibu, for one
4 Toothy tools
8 Water ___
12 Tuna in sushi
13 "Correct"
14 Don Juan's mother
15 LEGEND
17 Student's minor headache
18 It's often conducted on a couch
19 ___ Galore (Bond girl)
20 "The Incredibles" family name
21 Social worker?
22 From, datewise
24 Reason for Febrezin'
26 Busy person during tax season: Abbr.
29 LEGEND
32 Picnic invader
33 Painting materials
34 Board game with a "Castle" version
35 Go (for)
36 Matt who pitched a perfect game in 2012
38 They're usually blue
41 "Get the stick, boy!"
44 Shaft
45 LEGEND? (Think about it)
46 MasterCard rival
47 "Do ___ others ..."
48 Boston brew, familiarly
49 "Up and ___!" (Radioactive Man's phrase)
50 Sticky situation
51 Cardinals or Blues, for short

DOWN
1 Huck Finn's ride
2 "We have a problem"
3 Regularly seen item on a highway
4 Long-necked instrument
5 Good way to sell things
6 Not likely to be fooled
7 Chicago-to-Atlanta dir.
8 Resentment
9 What an albatross might symbolize
10 Hawaiian strings?
11 Famous bat head biter
16 NFL owner who gave Putin a Super Bowl ring
19 Salon job
21 Eagles, e.g.
22 In the style of
23 Big offense
25 Improvement over dial-up, for short
26 Simple thing to bet on
27 "I'd appreciate it," in chatrooms
28 "Fire away"
30 "My bad"
31 Provide with information
35 Late bedtime
37 Blaxploitation styles
38 Internet game format, possibly
39 "No ___" (Sartre classic)
40 As well
41 Out of the park
42 Paint layer
43 Web page standard
45 "This is delish!"

1	2	3	■	4	5	6	7	■	8	9	10	11
12			■	13				■	14			
15			16					■	17			
18							■	19				
■	■	20				■	21			■	■	■
22	23			■	24	25			■	26	27	28
29				30					31			
32			■	33				■	34			
■	■	■	35			■	36	37			■	■
38	39	40			■	41					42	43
44				■	45							
46				■	47				■	48		
49				■	50				■	51		

Solving enough puzzles to learn the styles of different constructors may prove helpful.

ANSWER, PAGE 95

TOOL TIME

ACROSS

1 When you'll probably take off: Abbr.
4 ___ 51
8 Suave guy?
12 Insurance payments
14 Grandchild in Genesis
15 Tasty tightener?
16 They get programmed before people go out
17 Clothing hybrid
18 Tater Tots maker
20 "Alas!" accompaniment
23 Backside, in Britain
24 Jagged fastener?
29 Brian who co-produced U2's "Joshua Tree" album
30 Candles' indication
31 Popular vacation destination, familiarly
32 Woodworker's affirmation?
37 Part of N.B.
38 Reptile that sounds unbelievable?
39 Writing surfaces
41 Tennis surface
45 "The Music Man" setting
46 Hosting carpenter?
49 Shout to a thief
50 "Deep Impact" star
51 "Lost" location
52 Flippable fad, once
53 ___ au vin (chicken cooked in red wine)

DOWN

1 Actor Omar
2 "Star ___"
3 Like the Empire State Building
4 "True, huh?"
5 Plate crossing
6 Ostrich relative
7 Regarding
8 Echo effect
9 Canines' neighbors
10 Little sister of Goneril and Regan
11 Greek peak
13 Friend of Broflovski, Cartman, and McCormick
19 Newspaper, to detractors
21 Chew, beaver-style
22 Soprano's showy note
24 Garland given as a gift
25 Items in some tests
26 Left the base, maybe
27 Hot, in a game
28 Drag
33 Like some Nixon conversations, famously
34 Not imposing
35 Wrecks beyond repair
36 Start of an ancient boast
39 Enthusiastic Spanish reply
40 Outgoing e-mail inits.
42 Popular guy at a univ.
43 Jay with a big jaw
44 La Salle of "ER"
47 Bus. driver?
48 Witch

You can get some warning about what sort of

1	2	3	■	4	5	6	7	■	8	9	10	11
12			13					■	14			
15								■	16			
17					■	■	18	19				
■	■	■	20		21	22	■	23				■
24	25	26					27					28
29			■	■	30			■	■	31		
32			33	34				35	36			
■	37				■	38				■	■	■
39					40	■	■	41		42	43	44
45				■	46	47	48					
49				■	50							
51				■	52				■	53		

theme, fill, and/or difficulty you're about to encounter.

ANSWER, PAGE 95

DEEP-SIXED

ACROSS

1 Ford model, or a homophone of what this puzzle is
3 Raise in relief
6 Bad thing to cross
8 Not completely
9 "It doesn't matter which"
10 Render useless, as a credit card
11 French restaurant worker
12 Dangers
13 It's blown in anger
14 "___ do, pig"
15 One who sticks to tradition
16 "Under Siege" actor Steven
17 Wear away
19 Word said right before a click
21 Mixing effect
23 Major road
26 Stocking dealer
28 Role for Alec or Ewan
29 Not as bright
30 "___ noches"
31 Poetic rhythms
32 Blunder or joke
33 Mexican-influenced music
34 Circumference / 2π
35 Decent
36 Hardly meek
37 Futuristic author
39 Artistic challenge in a children's magazine

DOWN

2 Looks self-satisfied
4 Peloponnesian War victor
5 Armpit, or a Phish song
7 "And so on and so forth": Abbr.
9 Simplified
10 Far from ample
11 Place to grow
12 It stuns
13 Juice sources
14 Be about to tip over
15 Antebellum
16 World ___
18 Pickling solutions
20 Company involved in gamesmanship?
22 Himalayan nation
24 Welcome message in a fighting game
25 Caviar source
27 Foreshadowed
29 Second sight?
30 People, so to speak
31 Part of ROM
32 "NCIS" actor Mark
33 Storm
34 Oyster place
35 Break
36 Boy in a 1976 horror film
38 Enjoy a sunny day, say
40 Flying off the shelves

Constructors sometimes like to make pangrams,

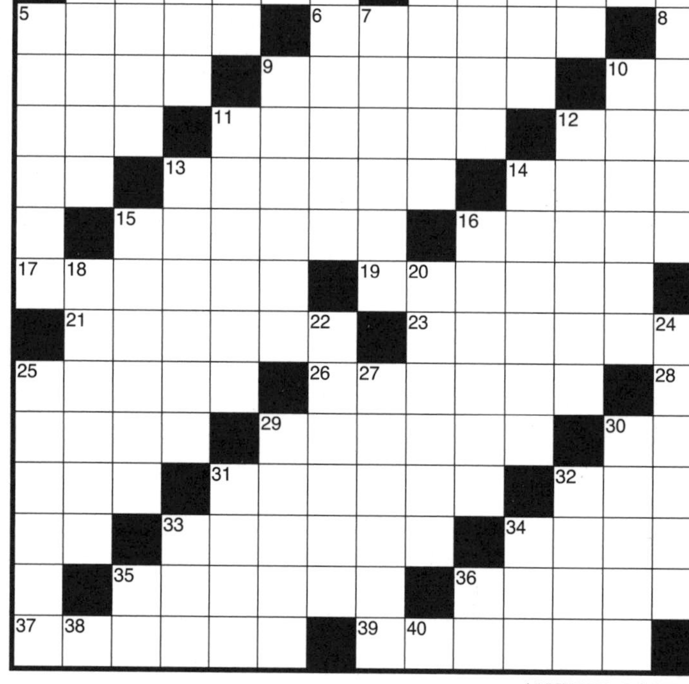

which are puzzles that contain every letter of the alphabet in their answer.

ANSWER, PAGE 95

THEMELESS CHALLENGE 8

ACROSS

1 Projects
5 Title for Horatio Magellan Crunch
9 It may cause a blow-up
12 Right away: Abbr.
13 Round do
14 Sneaky laugh
15 Doesn't hit a red light, say
18 Like a well-received meal
19 Ender's creator
20 Merci, in Munich
22 Seeing stars
24 Frequent booing target
25 "I Heard They Suck Live!!" band
27 "A Beautiful Mind" subject
30 What I try to put into my puzzles
33 Parking garage sign
34 Trap, in a way
35 Nature's clothes dryer
36 Good with pick-ups
38 Han's friend, at first
40 "Count me out"
42 "Huh"
44 Where imperial pounds are measured?
48 Ram partner
49 ___ contendere (court plea)
50 "Zounds!"
51 Feather bed?
52 Shockers
53 Locks (up)

DOWN

1 Where to find a lot of honking
2 Chant for Herb Brooks's team
3 Held like a hostage
4 "___ up!"
5 Travolta's "Face/Off" foil
6 Bittersweet thing to bid
7 Seasoned veteran
8 Sandman repellent?
9 Modern times
10 Animated clownfish
11 Common segue word
16 Note taker
17 Nine Inch Nails founder Reznor
20 Defrauded one
21 NASDAQ's partner
23 Grease target, maybe
26 Newsworthy, say
28 Tried to beat the ball
29 Long meal
31 Went 0 for 5 with two errors, say
32 World Baseball Classic supporter
37 Observe Yom Kippur
39 Where van Gogh painted "Sunflowers"
40 "Su-u-u-u-u-u-ure"
41 Drink, to a toddler
43 Grandson of Eve
45 Adversary
46 Slangy "no"
47 Driller: Abbr.

If you're really stuck on that final corner, and you see that the puzzle is, say, a Z away from the pangram,

see if anything jumps out at you when you mentally place a Z in one of your blank boxes.

ANSWER, PAGE 95

LUCK O' THE IRISH

ACROSS

1 Radio alerts of a sort: Abbr.
5 Anjou's relative
9 Cheerleader's asset
12 A host might invite you to take one
13 Field of expertise
14 Actress Gardner
15 Cruiser
17 Possible domain name ending
18 It's difficult to see through
19 Progenitor
21 Life's difficulties, in slang
23 Uniqueness
24 Org. symbolized by a staff of Aesculapius
25 Council Bluffs resident
26 Invention describer
32 Former NFLer Bernie
33 Emulate Eminem
34 Batter's sticky stuff
37 Ones with their noses in the air
39 Put up with
40 Segue word
41 Metal formerly called stannum
42 Like some quilts
46 Verb suffix
47 The first step
48 One branching out?
49 "That Was a Crazy Game of Poker" band, familiarly
50 "... which nobody can ___"
51 Foxy

DOWN

1 Shakespearean snake
2 ___ green
3 You step on it after getting clean
4 Subway stabilizer
5 "American Psycho" star
6 Aggressive Tolkien character
7 Nation with a strong navy
8 Desert travelers, collectively
9 "To Tell the Truth" group
10 Short-lived NBC series, with "The"
11 McDonald's unit
16 Lb. divs.
20 Tear to ribbons
21 You can stand to lose it
22 She was introduced to Oprah in a David Letterman joke on the Oscars
23 Like stock without a face value
25 "See you then!"
27 Barely got, with "out"
28 Place to jot down ideas
29 Hematite, for one
30 Collar
31 Smartphone feature, briefly
34 Barbecue's locale, often
35 Resort island near Majorca
36 Raider's local rival, popularly
37 "The baby is sleeping!"
38 Salamandridae members
40 Frozen treat chain
43 2,000 pounds
44 Oedipus ___
45 Crucial

If you're having trouble filling in that last square,

solid knowledge of etymology can be advantageous.

ANSWER, PAGE 95

THINK DIFFERENT

ACROSS
1 Balls (up)
5 O'er and o'er again
8 Like some coffee
12 Length × width, for a rectangle
13 Poet who was raven mad?
14 Closer's success
15 Ship navigation tool from Apple?
17 ___ school
18 Harmful cigarette stuff
19 "Unbelievable!"
21 William Phelps ___ (inventor of the stop sign)
22 Make one
24 Able
26 Pressure source
27 They take place in circles
29 Where to plug in an Apple device?
31 Feeling that has inspired a lot of soulful music
34 One of Pooh's hundred
38 Share, as a secret
39 Spanish pronoun for girls
40 Corrida shout
41 Row of tollbooths
44 They often contain emoticons
45 Comedian Richard
47 Spanish slang dictionary from Apple?
49 Hill occupants
50 Tuck's partner
51 "The Voice" host Carson
52 Game theorist John
53 Mag heads
54 They've split

DOWN
1 Shout from a slow child, maybe
2 Not widely known
3 Grandmother's affectionate term
4 Drain
5 Iridescent gem
6 20-Down relative
7 Hamilton
8 AOL or MSN
9 Mailing label words
10 Regardless of whether
11 Bus stations
16 Playoff impossibility
20 6-Down relative
23 Cleveland team, in headlines
25 Wreck
27 It has a plate at one end and a pole at the other
28 It may be in the hole
30 Response to freshness
31 Brand name in a drugstore
32 Northwestern capital
33 Olympic series
35 Gripping part of a story
36 Speak about nothing
37 English class submissions
39 Cranial wave catcher
42 Niacin, for one
43 Hits, in laser tag
46 Sorta: Suffix
48 Lemon or lime drink

Latin or Greek roots may lead you to the missing letter.

Likewise, considering English cognates may allow you to fill in a foreign word.

ANSWER, PAGE 95

PLACES, PLEASE

ACROSS

1 Computer that originally came in Bondi Blue
5 Word before highness or honor
9 Dodge model
12 Nothing to write home about
13 Flowing hair
14 Canadian boy on "South Park"
15 1984 Val Kilmer parody
17 Triumphant card player's statement
18 British rapper born Mathangi Arulpragasam
19 Vedic deity
21 It's written in a ratio
24 The H in his name stands for Henry
25 Archvillain in the video game God of War
26 Places for reds and whites
29 Tripping caller
30 Southern lady
31 Try to win
32 ___ stove
34 "Born from jets" brand
35 Tests without writing
36 "I can't catch a break!"
37 Idiot ___
39 "Got it!"
40 Lumberjack's implement
41 Hit the nadir
46 Sea, in the Sorbonne
47 West who played Batman
48 Doing
49 Golf's "Big Easy"
50 Large amounts
51 "Don't move, doggie!"

DOWN

1 Philosopher's suffix
2 Cow's sound, in cartoons
3 Snake in "Antony and Cleopatra"
4 Sagan series
5 Village People hit still popular at sporting events
6 Something to stick in the water
7 Without consistency
8 One withdrawing from a 401(k)
9 "No time to waste!"
10 Related (to)
11 File or Edit
16 One, for Ulf
20 Have a good cry
21 Be crabby
22 Treat often twisted apart
23 Reheated food
24 Unpleasant people
26 Wealthy
27 Don't stick around
28 Lifewater maker
30 Hacky Sack, essentially
33 Victoria's Secret sale, often
34 Tec
36 Guess ___? (kids' guessing game)
37 "As do I"
38 Lutz relative
39 PIN requesters
42 It might be picked up
43 Decline further correspondence, with "out"
44 Actress Hagen
45 Mess (with)

Bored by being able to write in

any answer as soon as you get it?

ANSWER, PAGE 95

CROSS WORDS

ACROSS

1 ___ card (phone insert)
4 Little insult
7 He called the 2002 MLB All-Star Game a tie
12 Is, for you
13 Valuable underground find
14 Ghana's capital
15 Base country for the Barbary pirates
17 Sing high notes?
18 AX
20 Cryptozoology figure
21 Moved smoothly (through), as a swimmer
25 Instant Messenger co.
27 College Football Hall of Famer Parseghian
28 Take advantage of
29 EX
33 Any belief
34 Be able to laugh at, as a joke
35 Storyline extending through multiple episodes
36 Have a scrap
38 Mayberry drunk
41 OX
45 Unconcerned, apparently
48 Encircling light
49 Name before noir or blanc
50 Better half, briefly
51 Beatty who voiced Lotso in "Toy Story 3"
52 2, 4, 6, etc.
53 Insults might hurt it
54 Pig's place

DOWN

1 Bided one's time
2 "Go me!"
3 Soldiers
4 San ___ (Silicon Valley city)
5 Extremely dry
6 Eliminate, maybe
7 "I'm out"
8 Danger from raw chicken
9 Watch readout, briefly
10 Vitriol
11 Square dance participant
16 It's not to be taken literally
19 Plant sometimes served fried
22 Computer programmer's chunks
23 Needle pt.?
24 "___ Rosenkavalier"
26 They strengthen the abs
27 Well-put
29 Toned
30 Sch. whose name officially starts with "The"
31 Rod's partner
32 Treasure's locale
37 Be overcome by handsomeness
39 Branch of the sea
40 Not reputable
42 Notre ___
43 Town's ending, at times
44 Roughly
45 Take after
46 Actress Tyler
47 Number in the upper left corner of most crossword grids

Diagramless crosswords require you to figure out

the grid pattern just from the clues and their numbers.

ANSWER, PAGE 96

THEMELESS CHALLENGE 9

ACROSS

1 Bob who guest-starred on "Home Improvement"
5 Send regrets, say
9 Econ. measure
12 "Lake Placid" villain
13 Play to ___ (draw)
14 "Cidade Maravilhosa," familiarly
15 Envelope words
18 Characteristic
19 Get to
20 Momentum
22 German military menace
24 Pitch
25 "In that case ..."
27 Sister and wife to Osiris
30 Eighth president of the NRA
33 Still a bit buggy, probably
34 Conglomerate in a 2002 scandal
35 JFK alternative
36 Steel girder named for its cross-section
38 Eric Stratton's "Delta House" nickname
40 Its prime factorization is CCCXXXI × V
42 Exposition in the Austin Powers films
44 Rally, perhaps
48 Defarge, e.g.: Abbr.
49 Well-known African flower
50 Chain that serves meatballs
51 Mr. ___ (stadium character)
52 Lip
53 Time spent at the DMV, it feels like

DOWN

1 Taper?
2 Emotion during a fit
3 Cheap but potentially extremely valuable item
4 Honda's luxury brand
5 Indian royalty
6 Yachts, jewelry, etc.
7 Kid ___ (Saturday morning fare)
8 Martinez with three Cy Young Awards
9 Big body of water with no fish
10 It may be slipped
11 Wife of Becks
16 "Caddyshack" director
17 What scripted shows do during a writers' strike
20 Reentry requirement, maybe
21 Raconteur's staple
23 Brownish pear
26 Greek salad topper
28 Brandon of the Oakland Athletics
29 "ET" subject
31 Fur-yielding mammal
32 Grey ___
37 Dale who married Roy Rogers
39 Fibula's neighbor
40 "This is delicious!"
41 Knight's female equivalent
43 Iowa State University site
45 "American Dad!" workplace
46 One who might go undercover on "Undercover Boss"
47 Kal ___ (pet food brand)

Looking to reach beyond the conventional crossword answers?

Try vowelless crosswords, in which you write only the consonants into the grid.

ANSWER, PAGE 96

ON TOP OF THINGS

ACROSS

1 Words that may be intr.
4 It's filled with twenties
7 Poetic preposition
11 Slightest bit
13 1995 Green Day song
14 Leader
15 Gooey lump
16 Actor Howard of "Iron Man"
18 Arrives
20 Snowy ___
21 World-weary fellow?
22 Passwords are associated with them
24 Family reunion attendee
25 Electronic music format
26 Road race, often
27 Moon and Starr, for two: Abbr.
28 Eat well
32 Oscar nominee for "Leaving Las Vegas"
34 English class assignment
35 Defeat, in Risk
38 Sierra ___
39 Pelvis part
40 Kitchen fixtures
42 Star of "The Aviator"
44 Don't bail on
45 Penultimate fairy tale word
46 Fallopian tube travelers
47 ___'acte
48 Still mooing, so to speak
49 Be joined
50 "Got it?"

DOWN

1 Like loud colors
2 Western ornament
3 German cake
4 Italian region noted for its wine
5 It's on top of this answer
6 View from the Riviera
7 It's on top of this answer
8 Artist Matisse or Toulouse-Lautrec
9 Moved fast
10 Playwright Clifford
12 It's on top of this answer
17 Saxophone player's purchase
19 Not quite straight down: Abbr.
23 "Pretty sneaky, ___!" (catchphrase in a Connect 4 ad)
27 "___ Sera, Sera" (Doris Day song)
29 Shapes with equal angles
30 Girl twice denied in a musical?
31 Something people want torn down
33 Good thing to get over
34 New Haven collegian
35 Mulled drink
36 Tony of the Minnesota Twins
37 More congenial
41 Path
43 Tiff

Thus, you can't tell at a glance how many letters

an answer has, just how many consonants it contains!

ANSWER, PAGE 96

TOO MANY SIDES

ACROSS

1 Quick punch
4 Walk of Fame feature
8 Sorts of resorts
12 Mrs., in Madrid
13 Give a thumbs-up on Facebook
14 West Virginia's Backyard Brawl opponent, popularly
15 Dangerous area for travelers?
18 Garb
19 Go to bed
20 Breakfast brand
21 High-scoring game
23 Rabbit relatives
25 Like some vbs. or mdse.
26 Texting protocol inits.
27 Alternate title for this puzzle
30 Fill, as an apartment
33 Android Market purchase
34 The Beatles induced one
38 How people gasp, often
41 "Yesterday" or "Tomorrow"
42 Not mono
43 Apt
45 New York tourist spot?
47 "So ..."
48 Korbut of Olympic fame
49 Certain logic gate
50 Suffix for many nouns
51 Portmanteau in a weather report
52 What's served in spots?

DOWN

1 Mass producer, for short
2 First name in soul music
3 Cash-free deal
4 Say indistinctly
5 They come in and go out
6 Letters before a nickname
7 Recycle bin option
8 Little rush
9 "Dueling" instruments
10 Blood flows through it
11 Blood flows through them
16 Gets along well
17 Business meeting need
22 Big zoo attraction
24 Is kind, in preschool
28 Apt
29 Little Italy offering
30 "Do you hear that?"
31 Whole
32 Booker T's band
35 Snickers ingredient
36 Chant
37 Business meeting need
39 They may be crushed in sundaes
40 2011 animated film starring Johnny Depp
44 How a single guy might go
46 Massachusetts state tree

Looking to reach beyond the conventional crossword clues?

You might try cryptic crosswords.

ANSWER, PAGE 96

KEYWORDS

ACROSS

1 "Take a ___ out of crime" (slogan of McGruff the Crime Dog)
5 Advanced deg.
8 Two-Buck Chuck, for one
12 High-flying mil. branch
13 "Yes, Yvette!"
14 Irish New Age singer
15 Inability to capitalize letters?
18 General ___ (car in "The Dukes of Hazzard")
19 Five of a kind, in a dice game
20 Melting point?
23 Charlottetown's prov.
24 Committee concerned with copying and pasting?
28 German conjunction
29 It might lead to a shootout
30 Two, in Tijuana
32 One cleverly exiting a dialog box?
37 Sports org. with a fifty-yard field
38 Searched, as a pig for truffles
39 Laundry treatment
43 Part of a great cost?
44 The right side of the keyboard?
48 "Hairspray" character Turnblad
49 Prefix with color
50 Enjoying
51 Newborn on the ranch
52 Total dump
53 "___ noted"

DOWN

1 Elementary schooler's ride
2 Book end?
3 Last remnants
4 Word after butterfly or Doppler
5 One in Washington
6 Cartoon duck with a red shirt
7 What many props in a magic show do
8 Entered
9 Big 1966 hurricane
10 It gets its bell rung
11 Facility
16 Glum drop
17 Citi Field replaced it
20 Hosp. part
21 Driving school staple
22 They're illegally grown
25 Don't just bend the truth
26 40-Down is under it
27 Fall short
31 Norm: Abbr.
33 Permitting jeans, say
34 Get an ___ effort
35 Not home, as a game
36 Like some love affairs
39 Choice, for short
40 26-Down option
41 It bursts in Sicily
42 Mario ___ (popular video game series)
45 "This Old House" pursuit, briefly
46 Rival of CIN and CHC
47 Word before sauce or milk

These imports from Great Britain have wordplay in their clues in addition to normal clues.

They're very satisfying to figure out!

ANSWER, PAGE 96

PHONOUNS

ACROSS

1 Really easy ones
8 Wagon parts
13 Appropriately shared
14 A split makes it difficult
15 The constructor follows someone around?
16 "You might enjoy this!"
17 Easternmost Arabian Peninsula country
18 They're sometimes hazel
19 Debate specification
21 The whole thing
22 Betting phrase that sounds like an oxymoron
24 Treebeard and kin
28 Speak ill of
29 The constructor and the solver chomped?
31 Assent asea
32 If's follower, in a computer program
34 Like some tomatoes
36 Pub pastime
38 One using a free disc that came in the mail, maybe
39 Good way to pay a bill
42 Feeling pretty good about oneself
43 Baby's bother
44 The solver rotates?
47 Potential partygoer's online receipt
48 Hall of fame?
49 Woodland deity
50 Starts to irritate

DOWN

1 Big econ. indicator
2 Org. with many unhappy returns
3 Goners
4 Really stuff
5 Totally freaked out
6 Word with collar or jacket
7 Horror franchise whose 2010 edition was in 3-D
8 Andy Pettitte or Roger Clemens, once
9 Foundation that gives awards for technological innovation
10 PepsiCo potato chip brand
11 Lakeside Pennsylvania city
12 Match parts
18 Golf announcer's cry
19 It contains the cerveau
20 The ___ Office
21 Milieu for the Clio Awards
23 "Faust" character
25 Hammers' replacements, perhaps
26 Compose, as e-mail
27 Crystal ball gazer
30 Olympics powerhouse
33 Balance sheet amount
35 Modem's neighbor
37 Manifestation of stress
39 Puts away
40 PBS science show
41 Dart (around)
42 Bitter
44 Y-axis : pitch :: Z-axis : ___
45 Duran Duran hit
46 Start to stop?

ANSWER, PAGE 96

PLAY BY PLAY

ACROSS

1 19th Greek letter
4 Games magazine publisher
9 "I am," in Latin
12 Mischief maker
13 Just perfect
14 23rd Greek letter
15 It's a tense situation ...
18 Coffee drinker's supply
19 Dragon-slaying saint
20 "You got it!"
23 "Today" weatherman
24 A penalty sets them back ...
26 Mined finds
27 One of ten
28 Nook Tablet alternative
32 He finds an open receiver ...
34 San ___, California
38 Plays in an upbeat fashion
39 Embodiment of wisdom
41 They get along
42 And to win ...
46 Forrest's portrayer
47 The Man's partner, in a '70s TV show
48 Paisley prize, for short
49 Suffix with crossword
50 Take effect
51 It's inserted, then turned

DOWN

1 "Verily!"
2 Words ending some autobiography titles
3 It turns towards the top
4 Sex studier
5 Toss in
6 Word after snap or snow
7 Feeling of hunger or guilt
8 Birch relatives
9 Camper's utensil
10 Grammarian's concern
11 Certain distance runner
16 Really mean people
17 Gross stuff
20 Money manager: Abbr.
21 Ancient Roman known as "the Censor"
22 Fisherman's target, at times
25 Style of the Chrysler Building
28 Dog collar attachment
29 Noted spatterer
30 Rockin'
31 It looks up IP addresses: Abbr.
32 Hair applications
33 Prepares to ride, as a motorcycle
34 Certain finish
35 Dumas character
36 Football, in this puzzle
37 Freaked-out shout
40 Rue the workout
43 Handy pack
44 Not there, in France
45 It starts at midnight

Puzzle books are great for airplane trips.

They won't be the target of theft and you don't have to close them during takeoff and landing.

ANSWER, PAGE 96

THEMELESS CHALLENGE 10

ACROSS

1 ___ Spiegel (German publication)
4 Robert ___
8 Dutch speedskater Kramer
12 Frequent star in Quentin's movies
13 Team that LeBron jilted
14 Skin care brand
15 Hit song on which two San Francisco 49ers sang backup
18 Name on chainsaws
19 Finish (out)
20 Up to
22 Wharton who created Ethan and Zeena
25 Early-21st-century health scare
27 Student's option
29 Nixon visited him in 1972
30 It's spoken at 45-Across
33 Shots from the charity stripe: Abbr.
34 Help to escape, say
35 Popular two-toned cookie
36 Scorpio's birthstone, usually
38 Bad waiter's comeuppance
40 Praiseful poet
42 Like some Siberians
45 The Long Walk leads up to it
48 "Or ___ what?"
49 Base for some brandy
50 Martinique is one
51 Wasn't colorfast
52 Daughter of Cronus
53 Rival of ATL and PHI

DOWN

1 Interjections from the intellectually insulted
2 Send off
3 Kind of team on an ambulance
4 Food poisoning cause
5 It may be yellow or chocolate
6 It looks the same in winter
7 Exxon's equivalent, in Canada
8 Like good reasoning
9 Leader who's an expert in judo
10 Van Gogh had one
11 Name rhymed with "Guy" in a TV title
16 That's plural
17 Herman Wouk's captain
21 Accident investigators: Abbr.
23 "Don't ___ me, bro!" (2007 catchphrase)
24 Chocolaty Hostess treat
25 Apt. measure
26 Machine setting, maybe
28 "___ the Sons" (Talese book)
31 Some characters in "The Producers"
32 Some cloths cover them
37 Injected into the conversation
39 Beauty pageant prop
41 Next year's upperclassman
43 Italian coffee brand
44 Be overrun
45 The blogosphere is part of it
46 Unable to work, say
47 "The Price Is Right" prize, often

If you want your everyday solving

to be a bit more competitive,

ANSWER, PAGE 96

WIDE OPEN

ACROSS

1 Cape ___
4 Demeanor
8 Summer hrs. in San Diego
11 Controversial marathon runner Rosie
13 Ubiquitous disco hit
14 The Altar in the night sky
15 What the Joneses may inspire
16 Apollo, for one
18 Permanently affects
20 Look (through) frantically
21 Mascot for the Maryland Terrapins
23 Amazon IDs
24 Mtn. statistic
25 "___'Em In" (Wings song)
26 Linus has one, in "Peanuts"
31 To be, in Spain
32 Belarusian, for one
33 Member of a mid-1800s political party
36 Land
40 "I might not be able to handle all that"
42 Obviously want something badly
43 O.J. Simpson book with the subtitle "Confessions of the Killer"
45 Vodka brand
46 Election Day mo.
47 Eccentric
48 It's good to do things with it
49 Test with an analytical writing section: Abbr.
50 Rubik who invented an eponymous cube
51 Kyoto cash

DOWN

1 Family symbol
2 Precise scale measurement
3 Egomaniacs, it's said
4 Website where many musicians have pages
5 Make-up technique?
6 Plain color
7 Biblical name meaning "pleasure"
8 Biblical tale with a lesson
9 Friday show
10 Least likely to offend
12 Hay fever treatment
17 Baseball bigwigs, briefly
19 Sci-fi character whose first name is Hikaru
22 Definite article in Dresden
26 Paged
27 Tending to wear away
28 "Extreme Couponing" network
29 Big ale serving
30 Shakespeare's style
31 Okemo pastime
34 Spitball, say
35 Completely different from
37 Just peachy
38 Spur upward
39 Sitcom with a notable outing
41 Locker room feature
44 The referee calls it: Abbr.

look no further than PuzzleSocial on Facebook.

Challenge friends and try to make the leaderboard!

ANSWER, PAGE 96

PARTING WORDS

ACROSS

1 Newton ingredients
5 Some residue
8 Our predecessors
12 Computer program element
13 Don't fold
14 Second word shouted in a pool game
15 MP's worry
16 Inaugurates
18 FR UIT
20 ___ chi
21 Like some coordinates
24 Brief exercise
27 Pleased
30 The Golden ___
31 HO ME
34 Good comedian
35 Medicine bottle info
36 Prefix for the EPA
37 "Me, too!"
39 Throw's path
41 SEA SON
47 Successful one
49 Wheel's need
50 "Easy there!"
51 She's sheared
52 Sting
53 Homeowner's pride
54 Iceland-to-Ireland dir.
55 Telegram punctuation

DOWN

1 Dieter's enemy
2 Caucus site
3 Enforcer
4 Sound goo might make
5 Had at
6 Plies a needle
7 Dickens's Uriah
8 Involving logic only
9 Musical end
10 Yale student
11 Heir, most likely
17 One of a European group
19 Rides
22 Brother of Billy
23 Design anew
24 Jolts
25 Whence the Buckeyes
26 "Jolly well done!"
28 Shakespearean title word
29 Be at odds (with)
32 Like Thomas More's world
33 It may be helping
38 More than annoyance
40 Unpleasant people
42 Currier's partner
43 Evening broadcast
44 Sign in airplanes and theaters
45 Palo ___
46 Don't rot
47 Puncturing tool
48 Half a dance?

I find that sitting outside with a bunch of puzzles

1	2	3	4	■	5	6	7	■	8	9	10	11
12				■	13			■	14			
15				■	16			17				
18				19							■	■
■	■	■	20			■	■	21			22	23
24	25	26	■	27		28	29	■	30			
31			32					33				
34				■	35				■	36		
37				38	■	■	39		40	■	■	■
■	■	41			42	43				44	45	46
47	48							■	49			
50				■	51			■	52			
53				■	54			■	55			

is a fine way to spend a nice afternoon.

ANSWER, PAGE 96

ANSWERS

7 HARD AT WORK

A	H	S	■	A	R	C	H	■	D	I	C	E
M	E	N	■	D	I	R	E	■	I	C	O	N
B	L	O	O	D	C	U	R	D	L	I	N	G
L	I	R	A	■	O	Z	O	N	E	■	■	■
E	X	T	R	A	■	■	■	A	M	P	L	E
■	■	■	■	R	E	V	S	■	M	E	E	K
S	W	E	A	T	L	I	K	E	A	P	I	G
H	A	L	T	■	L	A	I	R	■	■	■	■
E	X	I	L	E	■	■	■	R	A	J	A	H
■	■	■	A	L	A	M	O	■	V	E	G	A
T	E	A	R	S	F	O	R	F	E	A	R	S
H	A	N	G	■	R	A	Z	E	■	N	E	T
E	R	I	E	■	O	T	O	H	■	S	E	E

8 TAKE A BOW

A	R	F	■	W	E	E	D	■	J	I	G	S
P	A	R	■	H	A	R	E	■	A	L	O	U
E	V	E	R	Y	T	I	M	E	I	S	E	E
X	E	N	O	N	■	N	O	C	L	A	S	S
■	■	Z	O	O	S	■	S	H	E	■	■	■
S	K	I	T	T	L	E	■	O	R	G	A	N
P	O	E	■	■	Y	A	M	■	■	U	G	A
A	I	D	E	D	■	R	I	D	D	L	E	S
■	■	■	U	R	L	■	R	E	E	L	■	■
R	E	C	L	A	I	M	■	B	L	I	M	P
A	R	R	O	W	S	I	Q	U	I	V	E	R
G	R	O	G	■	P	L	U	G	■	E	G	O
E	S	P	Y	■	S	K	I	S	■	R	A	P

9 KEEPING TRACK

E	S	A	U	■	E	C	O	■	A	S	K	S
M	A	L	T	■	M	A	R	■	P	L	E	A
I	M	S	O	F	A	R	B	E	H	I	N	D
R	E	O	P	E	N	■	S	W	I	M	■	■
■	■	■	I	R	A	■	■	E	D	D	I	E
A	T	L	A	N	T	I	S	■	S	O	N	G
B	O	O	■	S	E	C	T	S	■	W	I	G
U	R	N	S	■	S	E	R	P	E	N	T	S
T	I	G	H	T	■	■	E	O	N	■	■	■
■	■	S	E	E	S	■	A	O	R	T	A	S
I	T	H	I	N	K	I	M	F	I	R	S	T
R	O	O	K	■	E	V	E	■	C	I	T	E
S	E	T	S	■	W	E	D	■	H	O	O	P

10 AS EASY AS ...

S	R	I	■	N	A	S	A	■	T	A	P	S
P	U	N	■	E	R	I	C	■	A	S	I	A
A	B	C	D	E	F	G	H	I	J	K	L	M
■	Y	A	R	D	■	N	E	O	■	F	E	E
■	■	■	E	S	S	■	■	U	F	O	■	■
F	I	B	S	■	C	E	N	S	O	R	E	D
O	T	I	S	■	O	V	A	■	R	I	G	A
G	O	G	E	T	T	E	R	■	E	T	O	N
■	■	A	D	E	■	■	Y	E	S	■	■	■
U	M	P	■	A	T	E	■	L	A	O	S	■
N	O	P	Q	R	S	T	U	V	W	X	Y	Z
I	D	L	E	■	A	C	N	E	■	E	N	E
T	E	E	D	■	R	H	O	S	■	N	E	D

11 GOING DOWNHILL

D	O	S	■	R	O	B	■	M	A	P	L	E
O	U	T	■	I	R	A	■	A	L	I	E	N
G	R	A	Y	*	E	S	■	R	A	G	E	D
■	■	D	E	N	S	E	S	T	■	*	D	S
F	L	I	N	G	■	■	M	I	E	N	S	■
I	O	U	■	■	S	E	I	N	E	■	■	■
R	U	M	P	E	L	S	T	I	L	T	*	N
■	■	■	A	R	O	S	E	■	■	U	F	O
■	G	A	S	U	P	■	■	F	I	E	F	S
*	R	T	■	P	E	E	P	E	R	S	■	■
M	E	R	I	T	■	*	L	L	E	D	I	N
P	A	I	N	E	■	M	O	O	■	A	C	E
S	T	A	N	D	■	O	W	N	■	Y	E	W

*** = SKI**

12 KUDOS

A	T	O	M	S	■	S	P	A	■	P	E	A
T	A	R	O	T	■	E	L	M	■	R	A	T
E	X	T	R	A	■	W	A	Y	T	O	G	O
■	■	■	A	N	T	I	C	■	O	P	E	N
W	E	L	L	D	O	N	E	■	T	O	R	E
A	G	O	■	P	U	G	■	H	A	S	■	■
S	O	W	H	A	T	■	D	E	L	E	T	E
■	■	P	O	T	■	D	O	A	■	T	A	L
P	A	R	R	■	G	O	O	D	W	O	R	K
I	R	I	S	■	R	U	M	B	A	■	■	■
N	I	C	E	J	O	B	■	A	G	I	L	E
T	E	E	■	O	W	L	■	N	E	V	E	R
A	S	S	■	E	S	E	■	D	R	Y	E	R

13 OFFBEAT

S	H	E	■	L	A	B	S	■	J	E	S	T
L	A	G	■	A	L	E	C	■	E	X	P	O
A	N	Y	■	U	L	N	A	■	S	P	E	W
C	O	P	S	D	I	D	N	T	S	E	E	■
K	I	T	T	E	N	■	■	V	E	N	D	S
■	■	■	A	R	O	M	A	S	■	S	E	T
S	P	R	Y	■	N	E	T	■	S	E	R	A
A	R	E	■	B	E	A	T	I	T	■	■	■
W	A	S	T	E	■	■	E	Q	U	I	P	S
■	I	T	I	D	I	D	N	T	D	O	I	T
F	R	O	M	■	T	I	D	E	■	T	A	U
E	I	R	E	■	E	V	E	S	■	A	N	D
Z	E	E	S	■	M	E	E	T	■	S	O	Y

14 IN THE MONEY

E	B	B	■	S	A	T	S	■	N	E	R	O
P	A	L	■	T	I	R	E	■	O	R	A	L
I	C	E	■	A	L	I	T	■	M	I	K	E
C	H	A	N	G	E	O	F	P	A	C	E	■
■	■	T	E	E	D	■	R	I	D	■	■	■
W	H	I	R	■	■	P	E	T	■	S	K	I
T	E	N	D	E	R	H	E	A	R	T	E	D
O	R	G	■	V	I	I	■	■	I	A	G	O
■	■	■	S	I	P	■	P	O	N	Y	■	■
■	B	I	L	L	O	F	R	I	G	H	T	S
J	A	D	E	■	P	O	O	L	■	E	R	A
A	L	O	E	■	E	R	N	E	■	R	A	N
Y	E	L	P	■	N	E	E	D	■	E	Y	E

15 APT ANAGRAM 1

A	D	S	■	W	O	E	S	■	N	A	S	A
N	O	T	■	A	L	M	A	■	O	D	O	R
T	W	E	L	V	E	P	L	U	S	O	N	E
E	N	V	O	Y	■	L	O	N	E	R	■	■
D	Y	E	S	■	E	O	N	S	■	N	E	T
■	■	■	S	E	X	Y	■	U	P	E	N	D
A	B	S	E	N	T	■	E	R	O	D	E	S
M	O	I	S	T	■	E	W	E	R	■	■	■
P	A	N	■	I	S	L	E	■	O	D	D	S
■	■	C	O	C	O	A	■	Q	U	E	E	N
E	L	E	V	E	N	P	L	U	S	T	W	O
G	O	R	E	■	A	S	I	A	■	E	E	R
O	X	E	N	■	R	E	E	D	■	R	Y	E

16 WE'VE GOT IT ALL

R	I	M	■	B	Y	T	E	■	A	L	M	A
O	D	E	■	R	O	O	K	■	T	E	A	R
B	O	R	N	I	N	W	E	D	L	O	C	K
S	L	E	E	T	■	■	D	U	E	■	■	■
■	■	■	G	I	S	T	■	B	A	W	D	Y
F	E	D	■	S	K	E	E	■	S	H	O	O
L	A	U	G	H	I	N	G	S	T	O	C	K
A	C	N	E	■	M	E	G	A	■	S	S	E
T	H	E	T	A	■	T	O	N	E	■	■	■
■	■	■	S	L	O	■	■	T	E	E	N	S
F	I	S	H	I	N	A	B	A	R	R	E	L
O	R	E	O	■	C	L	E	F	■	A	X	E
P	A	C	T	■	E	P	E	E	■	S	T	D

17 WHERE IT'S AT

A	R	M	S	■	A	M	I	■	S	E	L	F
F	O	A	M	■	N	O	D	■	T	R	E	@
L	U	G	E	■	A	L	A	C	A	R	T	E
@	T	I	L	@	H	E	H	U	N	■	■	■
■	■	■	T	O	E	■	O	D	D	J	O	B
A	S	K	■	N	I	A	■	■	P	O	K	E
R	U	N	@	E	M	P	E	R	@	U	R	E
K	E	E	L	■	■	T	A	O	■	R	A	P
S	T	E	A	M	S	■	S	S	T	■	■	■
■	■	■	N	O	M	@	T	E	R	W	H	@
A	S	I	T	W	E	R	E	■	O	R	A	L
D	C	V	I	■	A	I	R	■	V	E	R	A
D	@	E	S	■	R	A	N	■	E	N	D	S

18 APT ANAGRAM 2

H	A	Z	Y	■	J	A	B	■	A	M	P	S
A	L	E	E	■	O	N	E	■	T	E	A	L
N	O	E	L	■	U	N	S	T	E	A	D	Y
D	E	S	P	E	R	A	T	I	O	N	■	■
■	■	■	E	R	N	■	■	P	U	T	O	N
Q	U	A	D	R	A	N	T	■	T	I	D	E
U	N	I	■	S	L	U	R	S	■	M	E	X
I	T	R	Y	■	S	N	A	K	I	E	S	T
P	O	B	O	Y	■	■	D	I	N	■	■	■
■	■	A	R	O	P	E	E	N	D	S	I	T
W	A	L	K	W	A	Y	S	■	I	N	C	A
D	A	L	I	■	T	R	I	■	G	O	O	N
S	A	S	E	■	H	E	N	■	O	W	N	S

19 ON THE EDGE

YOUHAVEJUSTUT
G NILE ASIA I
NORMAN DERMAL
IVE STEER POI
NEST RED BENZ
ONTRIAL PUREE
S URL PER D
ABATE GRANDLY
EACH SRI TRIO
RBI HURON EMU
REDEEM READER
A IAMA TWIG P
LUCRICFOSREWO

The message around the edge of the grid reads: YOU HAVE JUST UTILIZED YOUR POWERS OF CIRCULAR REASONING.

20 APT ANAGRAM 3

ROAM REBA FIB
AREA ERAS ONE
PARR LIST RAG
SLOTMACHINES
HEX RESTS
AQUARIUS TEAL
RUN ENTER ETA
TELE GETUPSET
SNORT ASA
CASHLOSTINEM
PHD YOGI RAVE
GEE MOLD EVES
ADD EPEE DENS

21 THE SOUND'S THE SAME

MATED TAR LAG
EPOXY AMERICA
LETTERBEFOREZ
ORION BASE
PARR DODOS
EXIT ESSE AMP
WELSH RIVER
SSE EBBS NONO
SWEEP SNUG
AIDE CLASH
FORWHATREASON
AWESOME APPLE
RAW WED LEADS

22 LOOK THE OTHER WAY

TILPS GEK RAJ
ENERI OXE OGE
ENOON TIS UAE
TFELOTTHGIR
SYASSE REENS
PER TPAEL
YADSLOOFLIRPA
CINOT EID
LARUM ETADES
EGAMIRORRIM
NIK TAV ESEBO
ILE ECA SLAOF
NED DEL SETAF

23 READ ALL ABOUT IT

ETCH IRKS AGT
AHOY DEEP CUR
TAKECOVER IRA
SIENA SPEEDUP
ARK GEAR
CUP VITO RAMS
SPINECHILLING
ASTO KENO NOT
FURS GUY
PEANUTS SELMA
ALL MAPLELEAF
ILL BRIE LAZE
LAS ATNO SKEW

24 REREAD ALL ABOUT IT

RAJA SHOE SEE
ALIT LYNX CAR
NOVELIDEA AGO
CHE ODE LURED
HASAT ATTIRE
STEAL MELD
SECONDSTORY
CAVE DOORS
AMENDS ATLAS
MONTE BEL EMU
EVE BOOKAROOM
TAS TRUE ANNO
ORT SETS PEGS

25 THAT SPECIAL SUM THING

IAMB AWL STIR
THAI TOE THRU
TARGETED REAM
DRE GL+EN
AL+IN EEL
FRAYED SIERRA
DEW EON
RANDOM ATBEST
EWE TW+LE
BL+ER TAR
LIEU INASENSE
ALEC TRI ABEL
PERK SAN MAXI

26 2-H CLUB

ECRU NOVA KFC
SPUN ODES NEO
SASS WITHHOLD
HEMIN AXLE
CHAIN FDR
RIOTS SLAPPED
EAU UHHUH IRE
FORESEE LENIN
TEN WINCE
ALEC ROACH
FISHHOOK AHEM
AMP EAVE SITE
RAY WREN ETAL

27 CASE STUDY

JUST AND BEG
PRISM DOE LEI
GENOA STPAULS
LVE CUTEST
CHI EIGHTHS
RUNINTO YOKEL
ELAN ONE MIMI
WATTS ESTEEMS
RECURTO SAP
SHARON EPA
CONNOTE STEAM
ABC PIT YALTA
MOE SEA TIME

The message in the grid reads: JUST SOLVE IT ONE STEP AT A TIME.

28 CHRISTMAS EVE SCHEDULE

DATA WEB AWES
REAP ATA NOME
USSR STRUCKUP
GOTOCHURCH
SPEND LOOSE
SINGCAROLS
AHA AAH HOP
PUTOUTMILK
THEFT AIRES
FALLASLEEP
RAPSHEET LARA
ALOE AGO EDIT
NEXT FOP DYES

29 REARRANGEMENTS

ERAS PCT ELSE
TINY OAR MEAL
ACTS SPITBALL
HITTHEBRAKES
ERE EEL
BLEMISH MAIL
EEN STOWS BRO
LIDS CHOOSES
ENS ALP
PLANTHOLDERS
OUTSHONE NAIL
OBOE VER URGE
HEMS ESS PEND

30 PIECEWORK

HERR ASP AVOW
IDEA BEE LIMO
GNAW HAS LEEK
HARDCOREPAWN
EAR TOY
DFLAT OAK EDU
JAILHOUSEROOK
SAP OPT FENCE
ODE SUM
SILENTKNIGHT
BIND AYE NOAH
ONCE IRE DAZE
WEAR ROT STEM

31 SHIFT HAPPENS

```
APB■WAD■APHID
BAR■EGO■NOOSE
UNEATEN■NIGHT
GEAR■ONION■■■
■■KEPLER■TRIP
REF■ADDS■TIDE
APRIL■■■FOOLS
SEEM■ISLE■GET
PEEP■FLOWER■■
■■■ASSET■MAKE
STICK■ATTUNED
HAITI■ZOO■DEG
EXIST■ESP■ENE
```

32 OH, C, CAN YOU SAY?

```
PORK■VAST■FCC
SHOE■EXPO■LOU
IMMENSEAMOUNT
■■■PETS■BOXES
STRAW■■BOZ■■■
WHATTHEEYESDO
IAN■■AIR■■POX
MIDDLINGGRADE
■■■OAR■■AARON
AUDIT■COLT■■■
SPANISHASSENT
TOT■NEAT■OREO
ONE■OWNS■NATO
```

33 FIT TO BE TIED

```
CPA■JAYS■MOPS
AID■AWOL■ARIA
SQUAREDANCING
TULL■DAVE■FEE
SETIN■■■WAIFS
■■■■ALUM■SCOT
■SLIPOFPAPER■
GAEL■OOHS■■■■
RITES■■■KNOTS
ODS■OBOE■OPAL
WINDSORCASTLE
ODOR■MARX■IKE
NOTE■BLUE■CST
```

34 THAT'S THE SPIRIT!

```
JED■WASTE■*TH
AXE■ILLER■KIA
BAM*ZLING■KEN
SMOG■ETD■PERK
■■■IAN■ONCE■■
LIBEL■INASPOT
ERA■GHOST■ELI
TABLEAU■ACRES
■■YARN■ALA■■■
BA*N■GEM■BAM*
ULM■*STERSHOT
FOE■RUNNY■AVE
FUR■SPADE■BED
```

* = BOO

35 ON THE UP AND UP

```
JOT■FLAY■FROM
ERA■LOOM■RENO
FEE■YOKE■ANEW
FOMENT■NINA■■
■■DANG■ECZEMA
AGES■NONE■LAX
LOUT■IRA■ACRE
ETC■SNAP■FLED
CHEQUE■RARA■■
■■BUNT■EXOTIC
VERA■SATE■NOR
OKAY■ABEL■ETA
WEBS■FOPS■DAM
```

36 THEMELESS CHALLENGE 1

```
CAB■SLIP■ACME
LOU■CONE■GRIN
ONTHEOPENROAD
GETON■ARIES■■
■■ENTER■NESTS
TARO■VENN■EWE
EMERGENCYEXIT
NOD■ESTA■VANS
TITAN■HAREM■■
■■ONICE■ANITA
WHATELSEISNEW
HOSE■VEES■EAR
OPTS■ISLE■DRY
```

37 DON'T COUNT ON IT

```
CST■LOG■ASHES
AAA■IRA■STOLE
NUMBERS■PETIT
STEEL■PLIED■■
TERROR■ERRATA
■■■TWELVE■TOM
HIGH■DOE■DEEP
ECO■HEARYE■■■
NETPAY■SELLER
■■LANES■ATARI
CLOUD■PHRASES
MASSE■RUN■ICK
INTEL■YES■KTS
```

38 THREE-WAY TIE

```
AKA■■IAMB■CAB
CORD■OLAY■UFO
TAKESWING■TAX
ELISHA■SOLAR■
DANCE■■■NARCS
■■■■■MAKESURE
ABC■RINGS■GYM
DEADENDS■■■■■
VALID■■■FLIES
■CLEFT■PLINTH
SOS■LORDOFTHE
GNU■AREA■ERIE
TSP■GEMS■■OCT
```

39 ONE FOR THE EDITORS

```
CITY■CBS■SCAR
OMOO■HEN■HERE
GURU■REASONED
SPENDINGCUT■■
■■■GIS■SITARS
WIIMOTE■■■VIA
INSCRIBEDCOPY
ICI■■■BLOUSES
GATORS■BUR■■■
■■TOMATOPASTE
QUIZSHOW■CHUM
TAME■IKE■AUNT
REED■BED■ONES
```

40 APT ANAGRAM 4

```
MAID■BACH■OWE
ALTO■ABLE■PEZ
ROLLERCOASTER
CELLAR■ALASKA
■■■ASI■KEG■■■
QUARTET■RAJAH
URN■■RAD■■EGO
OLIVE■ROOFTOP
■■■ENS■USA■■■
SAFETY■BLUFFS
TERRORSLOCALE
ERA■MIKE■EDEN
POT■BAYS■TEXT
```

41 CLOWNING AROUND

```
EST■ACT■BITTE
THO■MOW■AWAIT
HOWDOYOUKILLA
EVERSO■TENK■■
RELY■TEE■■BOA
■■■IDEA■ORION
CIRCUSGORIGHT
DRIED■EBBS■■■
SAP■■ORS■IRKS
■■FOWL■CANINE
FORTHEJUGGLER
ADORE■ARE■ELF
DEMON■WED■STS
```

42 THEMELESS CHALLENGE 2

```
GAGA■ECRU■DNA
ELAN■CAIN■EUR
MAGNACUMLAUDE
■■GAMES■ELSES
BELLA■EDDIE■■
EVE■SAFE■AXLE
GOODSPORTSMAN
SOFA■ERNE■AND
■■GRETA■ROCKS
QUEEN■LURCH■■
ONEDAYATATIME
PTS■CORE■ANEW
HOE■TUMS■DATE
```

43 AFTER ONE TOO MANY ...

```
FINGER#SPRATS
ICEAXE#ELISHA
BUZZED#TANKED
###ACEKING###
ASP##YIN#SPEC
SMASHED#MORAL
CIRCUS#FRUITY
OLSEN#BLITZED
TEEN#PIE##ENE
###EMANATE###
WASTED#BOMBED
ANSWER#ADMIRE
STROKE#GOATEE
```

44 CRUNCH TIME

```
PUBS#JAMS#C[AB]S
ALOE#ERIC#OUI
INH[AB]IT[AB]LE#LTD
DARED#SANJOSE
###DEN#NEON##
PRE#SA[AB]##LIBS
EIGHTMINUTE[AB]S
TOGO##TOM#SEW
##ROTC#NBC###
S[AB]OTEUR#RIFFS
PAL#[AB]RACAD[AB]RA
ASL#ASIA#ELAL
YES#GENT#RENT
```

45 STRAIGHT FLUSHES

```
MID#AWHIR#JAB
IDO#SCENE#OVA
FEW#IFANDWHEN
FANMAIL#ION##
##TINE##NOSED
DAHL#LUCK#TOO
AXED#DNA#BENZ
NET#ASIN#RISE
GLOAT##IWON##
##INT#THISBIG
ILLNESSES#EDD
QUE#SHALE#CIA
SGT#TARPS#KEY
```

46 FROM THE MAILBAG

```
GTO#FATS#AHOY
OAR#DROPALINE
WHATACOOLIDEA
NOTI#HTTP####
SEESAW##SAGAS
####TALC#MAXI
I[L/H][O/A][V/T]EYOUTYLER
DUDE#SOBE####
OGDEN##ENRICH
####OPER#ANDY
THISISTOOHARD
NEVERSTOP#NOR
TREX#TUTS#EMO
```

30-Across has three squares with two answers, forming either LOVE or HATE.

47 MR. PUZZLE

```
TIP#APBS#KEGS
ONO#TROI#AGES
WASNTONTARGET
INSYNC#IDLY##
TEEM#ETNA#ODE
###PASO#GILES
LIGHTSPRINKLE
AFOOT#PEON###
DST#ASST#INCA
##OPIE#ANNEAL
ADVENTUREGAME
DEER#USDA#PER
JERK#PEST#SOT
```

48 THEMELESS CHALLENGE 3

```
BAR#TAPE#AFAR
ARE#OBIT#ROLO
JACQUESCHIRAC
ABOUT#THOSE##
##RASTA#RESIN
LCDS#ACTS#TSE
ORBITTHEEARTH
CAR#HAIL#LEOI
OBESE#OLLAS##
##ANTON#OMEGA
MAKEARUNFORIT
IDEA#ETAT#VGA
CORK#SSNS#EST
```

49 ON THE SLOPES

```
OUTS#OPIE#UPS
ANAL#ZEAL#RIP
SCHUSSAMINUTE
ILOSE##BOOGIE
SEEHERE#TRUED
####KING#MASS
##PISTEAWAY##
GRAD#EMMA####
AILED#YELLSAT
SPEARS##DENSE
SLALOMPROMISE
EEL#PURE#OPEN
DYE#STYX#NETS
```

50 FOUR EASY PIECES

```
MBA#GFS#SCHWA
PRIMERS#TOYED
HOLYCOW#RUPEE
###TKO##OPEDS
REDHOTPOKER##
ALAS##ROE#BET
JAR#CHIPS#OXY
ALT#ARE##SLIP
##BAKEDPOTATO
AROSE##ANA###
NAACP#UNICORN
ATRIA#SICKDAY
LEDIN#ACE#ETC
```

51 HOP TO IT

```
SST#ODDS#AMMO
QUO#BOAT#NEAT
URN#JUMPSTART
IFEVER##HINGE
RESET#BOOSTER
TRUE#SIRE####
#SPRINGBREAK#
####TUGS#RUED
DOGTAGS#WADER
ENROL##CASINO
LEAPYEARS#BEN
LAZE#SPUN#LYE
SLED#TEXT#YES
```

52 EXCHANGE PROGRAM

```
PILAF#AMP#GPA
SOUSA#BOTTLES
SWAPCLUESWITH
TAU#EAT##OBEY
###BMW#YES###
TIARA#VENISON
ACROSSANDDOWN
RETAKEN#RENEW
###DST#JED###
EASE##KOS#EMO
THESAMENUMBER
NEXTDAY#LABEL
AMY#DOS#TESTY
```

53 SIGN LANGUAGE

```
TIC#LUBES#OJS
XML#IRAQI#HAH
TAURUSRUN#ASA
#LEE#ARIESROD
SIDEA####KANE
EVILGEMINI###
ZEN#REAVE#MSG
###CANCERCAKE
ALDA####FADED
LEOTAMER#BOW#
TAZ#PISCESNET
EVE#BROAD#NRA
REN#SASSY#ASP
```

54 THEMELESS CHALLENGE 4

```
INCA#ASIA#LBJ
NEAP#VENN#ORE
DONTMENTIONIT
##ATARI#TWEET
ENDOR#ORALS##
DEI#CARE#ETNA
GRAPHICDETAIL
EDNA#DISC#RCA
##BIDET#OLSEN
DRANO#ISLET##
DOCTORZHIVAGO
ADO#RHEA#ETON
YEN#SONG#REDO
```

55 SPIT IT OUT

```
ASK#BAND#SWIG
MONGOLIA#LINE
FFORMALDDANCE
#ATOB##SAM###
####AIM#MIDST
POWERTIE#NILE
HHOLDINGTTOOL
AIRE#STGEORGE
TOMMY#YON####
###EIN##SUBS#
SSUNNYPPERIOD
POST#POPULACE
AXES#DEPP#SKI
```

56 WHY BOTHER?

```
SETS#ACH#AJAR
PAIL#MIA#CASA
FUTILEATTEMPT
##UPON#BISECT
WALKS#BOG#SAY
IVAN#FIXES###
ZEROTOZEROTIE
###TUXES#FROS
SEA#LIT#ATEUP
INVAIN#AREA##
SNAPPEDPENCIL
QUIP#SUE#ULNA
OILS#SOX#PEND
```

57 DOOR PRIZES

```
CAN#BRA#MAZDA
USO#LEX#IVIES
PASSAGE#CONCH
SPECIALTRICK#
##CURL#ROD###
SERB##JEN#SPA
TREATQUESTION
YET#HUG##EXIT
###LEI#WARP##
#TRICKORTREAT
CHINA#MELANIE
DEFER#NSA#CNN
SEEDS#ITS#ETD
```

58 NOT A SINGLE WORD

```
POP#CRAB#FIJI
EMIGRATE#ANON
SALLIEMA#LABS
ONEAM##CELS##
###SPAGHETTUS
SCISSOR#GOAPE
ART##LOP##TOW
GOSEE#WORSENS
ACAPPELLUM###
##LOAN##LEAVE
REIN#ANTILLIS
ENVY#COINTOSS
POEM#TVPG#TAO
```

59 SEE HERE

```
PDQ#USS#BEFIT
TRUSTEE#REACH
SEEKING#ARTIE
###ALDA#CIA##
ICETEA#SEESAW
PAGE#NLER#ALI
ANG#BOOMS#PIN
SOB#ETTE#KING
SEETHE#STAGES
##AWE#UTEP###
SATES#SEEPAGE
ALERT#MRMACHO
WARPS#ASS#TIN
```

60 THEMELESS CHALLENGE 5

```
LIL#MUTE#DRAB
AHA#OSHA#EURO
DOWJONESINDEX
SPOOL#BELIE##
##FLAME#OMAHA
CHAI#OATS#WON
LIVEINTHEPAST
OLE#NOGO#EKES
DORIC#ORATE##
##AMUSE#BINGE
FIGURESKATING
EVES#TOES#NAG
ZEST#ANNE#GTO
```

61 3×4

```
CAFE#ASP#BIB#
ALES#CHO#EDU#
NOTCUTOUTFOR#
STERN#OREO###
###ODE##ARTSY
#HOWOLDAREYOU
GOD##MOW##ROM
MOOGOOGAIPAN#
STRAW##YSL###
###ZEST#LADLE
#THESAYHEYKID
#LOB#SPA#ENVY
#CEO#HOG#RYES
```

62 O MY!

```
SHAQ#SWAG#ZIT
GURU#OHIO#OBI
THROWFORALOOP
##ATIT##LIMOS
JONES#TROTSKY
AUG##PRUNE###
WRESTLINGRING
###CHOPS##NEO
UMLAUTS#MADTV
PAIRS##TROY##
TRAFFICCIRCLE
OAR#ARAB#TAIL
PTS#RELY#ARTS
```

63 NOT QUITE

```
BBB#VPS#ASTRO
ELO#ARP#SPEAR
TOOTSIE#SIEGE
ACROSSCLUES##
###RAM#URL###
APRIL#WRESTLE
BUY##WOK##AAA
STEPSON#FIRST
###OAR#GOO###
##DOWNANSWERS
WOODY#CATALAN
HALLE#EWE#SPA
OTTER#SSR#ESP
```

Every Across clue has a typo, and every Down answer does, too.

64 THEMELESS CHALLENGE 6

```
DIMS#ATTA#LIZ
ENYA#GAIN#ONE
NEWYORKMINUTE
##INNIE#TOILS
DOFOR#SHARE##
ICE#YIPE#SAIL
STAGEPRESENCE
CONN#SILL#DOG
##DOJOS#OPENS
ASKME#OUTER##
QUIETONTHESET
UND#ELEE#LOGO
ASS#SARS#SNOW
```

65 COLLEGE YRS.

```
MYTH#LOCH#QBS
OSHA#OOHS#UAE
CLERGYMAN#ONE
##STRAPS#ATAD
SUPERLATIVELY
ONO###HERE###
BOTTLE#NECTAR
###AURA###OLD
EWINGINDALLAS
JOTS#TOOBAD##
ELS#MRINSPAIN
CFO#VENT#SLAY
TSK#PATS#ELMS
```

66 ROUND TRIP

```
SPAZ#SEAT#DDE
POPE#ARCH#REX
FIRSTFREE#AMP
###TOE##MAGOO
SWAYS#ONAIR##
PAL#SECONDAID
OSLO#CEO#ACNE
THIRDHAND#ERA
##SCION#RISEN
ATLAS##JAB###
ZOO#HOMEWORLD
IRS#EDIT#OHIO
ZIT#SETS#KOBE
```

67 UNBALANCED DIET

```
ATTA DEI ISLE
TERM OWN CAIN
ERIN DEGRADED
MIXEDGREENS
 SOY NOTOUT
ASTIR EUR NRA
SCRAMBLEDEGGS
POE OUI EASES
STATUS IRR
 TOSSEDSALAD
TOILETTE CEDE
BASE OTS HAZE
STET PUT EKED
```

68 SWEET!

```
ABOUT ADAMANT
DONHO DELILAH
DIFFICULTTIME
ELI LOB EAU
NERVES TAINTS
DREW NATASHA
 BAREXAM
CLAUSES BAJA
LAUGHS PASTOR
ITS ABS CSI
PITCHERSSPOTS
ONEPINT AISLE
NONAMES METES
```

69 KNOW THE RULES

```
AID SUBS LOOP
CORALSEA EZRA
TWOLINEPASSES
SAPID PBS
 BIDS BEEP
NOLINECHANGES
EMO MOI ALI
TAGUPOFFSIDES
 ROLL FITS
 CEO RINGS
HAVEASHOOTOUT
ODOR LEAPINTO
TOWS OPTS ESP
```

70 THEMELESS CHALLENGE 7

```
NEW PIPS MSGS
AVE IDIO EWES
SELFCONFIDENT
ALLOT SADIE
 QUOIT YATES
SHUN ORAL PLO
HEADSWILLROLL
URL TAPE ATAD
IBIZA EXTRA
 FESTS RETAX
JAILHOUSEROCK
AGED DICK ERE
YODA OTIS SOS
```

71 ONE FROM THE ARCHIVES

```
WON SLY DEPTH
OVA HEE IVANA
LETSEAT GISTS
FROMMVISITS
 APE INAFEW
CBER AFT APU
HAMMVICTORIES
ACE ETC ALES
SHRINE ELI
 GRIMMVIDEOS
ADIOS MIASARA
DUNNO VCR CEL
OBGYN ITS HOT
```

72 ONE FOR THE AGES

```
RUM SAWS POLO
AHI ITIS INEZ
FOLKTALE QUIZ
THERAPY PUSSY
 PARR BEE
ASOF ODOR CPA
LISTOFSYMBOLS
ANT OILS RISK
 OPT CAIN
JEANS GOFETCH
AXLE YOURFOOT
VISA UNTO SAM
ATOM MESS STL
```

73 TOOL TIME

```
ETD AREA RICO
PREMIUMS ENOS
PECANNUT VCRS
SKORT OREIDA
 SIGH ARSE
LIGHTNINGBOLT
ENO AGE RIO
IKNOWWHATISAW
 BENE CROC
SLATES TABLE
IOWA MCHAMMER
STOP TEALEONI
ISLE POGS COQ
```

74 DEEP-SIXED

```
 TAURUS EMBOSS
ARTLY MEDIAN P
XOUT EITHER MA
ILS GARCON PER
LL GASKET THAT
L PURIST SEAGA
ABRADE CHEESE
 REVERB ARTERY
BIWAN HOSIER O
ENAS DUMBER BU
LER METERS HOW
US TEJANO RADI
G HUMANE DARIN
ASIMOV DRAWME
```

The grid consists of only six-letter words, and as answers go off the grid on the right or bottom, they continue from the left or top.

75 THEMELESS CHALLENGE 8

```
JUTS CAPN TNT
ASAP AFRO HEH
MAKESGOODTIME
 EATEN ORSON
DANKE DAZED
UMP NOFX NASH
PERSONALSTYLE
EXIT TREE AIR
 SUAVE LANDO
IWONT WEIRD
BANKOFENGLAND
EWE NOLO EGAD
TAR EELS SEWS
```

76 LUCK O' THE IRISH

```
APBS BOSC PEP
SEAT AREA AVA
PATROLCAR NET
 HAZE PARENT
LUMPS NOVELTY
AMA IOWAN
PATENTPENDING
 KOSAR RAP
PINETAR SNOBS
ABIDED THEN
TIN PATCHWORK
IZE ATOB TREE
OAR DENY SEXY
```

77 THINK DIFFERENT

```
WADS OFT ICED
AREA POE SAVE
ICAPTAIN PREP
TAR ILLBE ENO
UNITE UPTOIT
PEER FACEOFFS
 ISOCKET
THEBLUES ACRE
REVEAL ELLAS
OLE PLAZA IMS
JENI ICARAMBA
ANTS NIP DALY
NASH EDS EXES
```

78 PLACES, PLEASE

```
IMAC YOUR RAM
SOSO MANE IKE
TOPSECRET GIN
 MIA VISHNU
COLON PEROT
ARES WINEBARS
REF BELLE WOO
POTBELLY SAAB
 ORALS WHYME
SAVANT AHA
AXE BOTTOMOUT
MER ADAM UPTO
ELS GOBS STAY
```

79 CROSS WORDS

S	I	M	■	J	A	B	■	S	E	L	I	G
A	R	E	■	O	R	E	■	A	C	C	R	A
T	U	N	I	S	I	A	■	Y	O	D	E	L
B	L	A	D	E	D	T	O	O	L	■	■	■
Y	E	T	I	■	■	■	K	N	I	F	E	D
■	■	A	O	L	■	A	R	A	■	U	S	E
F	O	R	M	E	R	P	A	R	T	N	E	R
I	S	M	■	G	E	T	■	A	R	C	■	■
T	U	S	S	L	E	■	■	■	O	T	I	S
■	■	■	W	I	L	D	B	O	V	I	N	E
A	L	O	O	F	■	A	U	R	E	O	L	E
P	I	N	O	T	■	M	R	S	■	N	E	D
E	V	E	N	S	■	E	G	O	■	S	T	Y

80 THEMELESS CHALLENGE 9

V	I	L	A	■	R	S	V	P	■	G	D	P
C	R	O	C	■	A	T	I	E	■	R	I	O
R	E	T	U	R	N	A	D	D	R	E	S	S
■	■	T	R	A	I	T	■	R	E	A	C	H
S	T	E	A	M	■	U	B	O	A	T	■	■
T	A	R	■	I	F	S	O	■	I	S	I	S
U	L	Y	S	S	E	S	S	G	R	A	N	T
B	E	T	A	■	T	Y	C	O	■	L	G	A
■	■	I	B	E	A	M	■	O	T	T	E	R
M	D	C	L	V	■	B	A	S	I	L	■	■
M	A	K	E	A	C	O	M	E	B	A	C	K
M	M	E	■	N	I	L	E	■	I	K	E	A
M	E	T	■	S	A	S	S	■	A	E	O	N

81 ON TOP OF THINGS

V	B	S	■	■	A	T	M	■	T	H	R	O
I	O	T	A	■	S	H	E	■	H	E	A	D
B	L	O	B	■	T	E	R	R	E	N	C	E
R	O	L	L	S	I	N	■	E	G	R	E	T
A	T	L	A	S	■	U	S	E	R	I	D	S
N	I	E	C	E	■	M	I	D	I	■	■	■
T	E	N	K	■	Q	B	S	■	D	I	N	E
■	■	■	S	H	U	E	■	E	S	S	A	Y
C	O	N	Q	U	E	R	■	L	E	O	N	E
I	L	I	U	M	■	F	R	I	D	G	E	S
D	I	C	A	P	R	I	O	■	G	O	T	O
E	V	E	R	■	O	V	A	■	E	N	T	R
R	A	R	E	■	W	E	D	■	■	S	E	E

82 TOO MANY SIDES

J	A	B	■	S	T	A	R	■	S	P	A	S
S	R	A	■	L	I	K	E	■	P	I	T	T
B	E	R	M	U	D	A	S	Q	U	A	R	E
A	T	T	I	R	E	■	T	U	R	N	I	N
C	H	E	X	■	S	H	O	O	T	O	U	T
H	A	R	E	S	■	I	R	R	■	S	M	S
■	■	■	S	H	A	P	E	U	P	■	■	■
L	E	T	■	A	P	P	■	M	A	N	I	A
I	N	H	O	R	R	O	R	■	S	O	N	G
S	T	E	R	E	O	■	A	S	T	U	T	E
T	I	M	E	S	P	E	N	T	A	G	O	N
E	R	G	O	■	O	L	G	A	■	A	N	D
N	E	S	S	■	S	M	O	G	■	T	E	A

83 KEYWORDS

B	I	T	E	■	P	H	D	■	W	I	N	E
U	S	A	F	■	O	U	I	■	E	N	Y	A
S	H	I	F	T	L	E	S	S	N	E	S	S
■	■	L	E	E	■	Y	A	H	T	Z	E	E
I	C	E	C	A	P	■	P	E	I	■	■	■
C	O	N	T	R	O	L	P	A	N	E	L	■
U	N	D	■	■	T	I	E	■	■	D	O	S
■	E	S	C	A	P	E	A	R	T	I	S	T
■	■	■	A	F	L	■	R	O	O	T	E	D
P	R	E	S	O	A	K	■	A	R	M	■	■
R	E	T	U	R	N	A	D	D	R	E	S	S
E	D	N	A	■	T	R	I	■	I	N	T	O
F	O	A	L	■	S	T	Y	■	D	U	L	Y

84 PHONOUNS

C	I	N	C	H	E	S	■	A	X	L	E	S
P	R	O	R	A	T	A	■	S	P	A	R	E
I	S	H	A	D	O	W	■	T	R	Y	I	T
■	■	O	M	A	N	■	I	R	I	S	E	S
T	O	P	I	C	■	A	T	O	Z	■	■	■
E	V	E	N	O	D	D	S	■	E	N	T	S
T	A	R	■	W	E	B	I	T	■	A	Y	E
E	L	S	E	■	V	I	N	E	R	I	P	E
■	■	■	Q	U	I	Z	■	A	O	L	E	R
I	N	F	U	L	L	■	S	M	U	G	■	■
C	O	L	I	C	■	Y	O	U	T	U	R	N
E	V	I	T	E	■	A	R	S	E	N	I	O
S	A	T	Y	R	■	W	E	A	R	S	O	N

85 PLAY BY PLAY

T	A	U	■	K	A	P	P	A	■	S	U	M
I	M	P	■	I	D	E	A	L	■	P	S	I
S	E	C	O	N	D	A	N	D	G	O	A	L
■	M	U	G	S	■	■	G	E	O	R	G	E
C	O	R	R	E	C	T	■	R	O	K	E	R
F	I	V	E	Y	A	R	D	S	■	■	■	■
O	R	E	S	■	T	O	E	■	I	P	A	D
■	■	■	■	T	O	U	C	H	D	O	W	N
M	A	T	E	O	■	T	O	O	T	L	E	S
A	T	H	E	N	A	■	■	P	A	L	S	■
T	H	E	K	I	C	K	I	S	G	O	O	D
T	O	M	■	C	H	I	C	O	■	C	M	A
E	S	E	■	S	E	T	I	N	■	K	E	Y

86 THEMELESS CHALLENGE 10

D	E	R	■	E	L	E	E	■	S	V	E	N
U	M	A	■	C	A	V	S	■	O	L	A	Y
H	I	P	T	O	B	E	S	Q	U	A	R	E
S	T	I	H	L	■	R	O	U	N	D	■	■
■	■	D	O	I	N	G	■	E	D	I	T	H
S	A	R	S	■	T	R	U	E	■	M	A	O
Q	U	E	E	N	S	E	N	G	L	I	S	H
F	T	S	■	A	B	E	T	■	O	R	E	O
T	O	P	A	Z	■	N	O	T	I	P	■	■
■	■	O	D	I	S	T	■	I	N	U	I	T
W	I	N	D	S	O	R	C	A	S	T	L	E
E	L	S	E	■	P	E	A	R	■	I	L	E
B	L	E	D	■	H	E	R	A	■	N	Y	M

87 WIDE OPEN

C	O	D	■	■	M	I	E	N	■	P	D	T
R	U	I	Z	■	Y	M	C	A	■	A	R	A
E	N	V	Y	■		P	R	O	G	R	A	M
S	C	A	R	S	■	R	U	M	M	A	G	E
T	E	S	T	U	D	O	■	I	S	B	N	S
■	■	■	E	L	E	V	■	■	■	L	E	T
■	S	E	C	U	R	I	T	Y		E	T	■
S	E	R	■	■	■	S	L	A	V	■	■	■
K	N	O	W		■	A	C	R	E	A	G	E
I	T	S	A	L	O	T	■	D	R	O	O	L
I	F	I	D	I	D	I	T	■	S	K	O	L
N	O	V	■	K	O	O	K	■	E	A	S	E
G	R	E	■	E	R	N	O	■	■	Y	E	N

The empty squares contain the words SPACE, BLANK, and NOTHING (from top to bottom).

88 PARTING WORDS

F	I	G	S	■	A	S	H	■	A	P	E	S
L	O	O	P	■	S	E	E	■	P	O	L	O
A	W	O	L	■	S	W	E	A	R	S	I	N
B	A	N	A	N	A	S	P	L	I	T	■	■
■	■	■	T	A	I	■	■	P	O	L	A	R
J	O	G	■	G	L	A	D	■	R	U	L	E
A	H	O	U	S	E	D	I	V	I	D	E	D
R	I	O	T	■	D	O	S	E	■	E	C	O
S	O	D	O	I	■	■	A	R	C	■	■	■
■	■	S	P	R	I	N	G	B	R	E	A	K
A	C	H	I	E	V	E	R	■	A	X	L	E
W	H	O	A	■	E	W	E	■	B	I	T	E
L	A	W	N	■	S	S	E	■	S	T	O	P

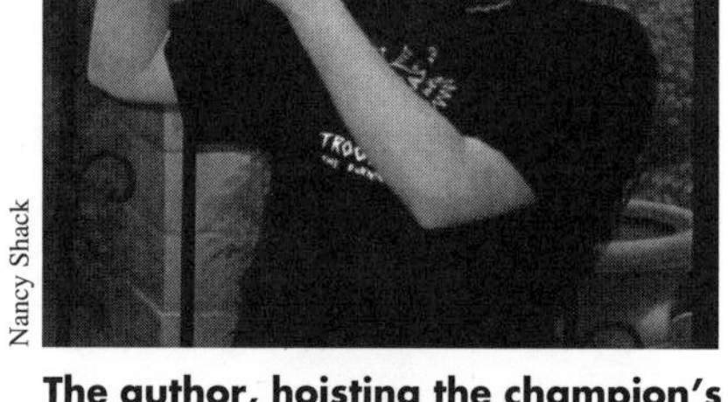

Nancy Shack

The author, hoisting the champion's trophy at the 2005 American Crossword Puzzle Tournament.